God's Pattern for Revival and Spiritual Awakening

FRESH ENCOUNTER

HENRY T. BLACKABY   CLAUDE V. KING

© Copyright 1993 • LifeWay Press
All rights reserved
Reprinted 1993, 1994, 1995, 1996, 1998

ISBN 0-8054-9920-2

Dewey Decimal Classification: 269.24
Subject Heading: Revivals

This book is the text for course CG-0117 in the subject area The
Church of the Christian Growth Study Plan. An application for
course credit is located in the back of the Leader's Manual or ask
your group leader to obtain a copy of Form 725.

Unless otherwise indicated, Scripture quotations are from The
Holy Bible, *New International Version*, copyright © 1973, 1978,
1984 by International Bible Society.

Printed in the United States of America

LifeWay Press
127 Ninth Avenue, North
Nashville, Tennessee 37234

Dear Colaborer,

Fresh Encounter represents more than a course of study. *Fresh Encounter* seeks to spearhead national revival and spiritual awakening, challenging churches to identify and overcome self-defeating habits and renew relationships with God.

The *Fresh Encounter* materials are designed for God's church, not a particular denomination. It is about knowing what it means to be God's people. Many denominations are presently using them. Sin is not confined to one denomination, it is an epidemic among all of our people. As a follower of Christ you have the answer. His name is Jesus. He is both salt and light. These materials lift Him up and will serve as a guide to motivate and mobilize your church.

May I encourage you to listen prayerfully to Henry Blackaby. God has anointed him to bring the message the church so desperately needs.

Henry speaks from experience. He has been with God. Expect God to do something big and count on revival breaking out in your midst. All of us know the fields are ripe unto harvest; the church is needy and revival must begin with us. God wants us to confess our sins, turn from our wicked ways, find out where He is working, and then join Him there all for His glory.

This will be the best day yet if we allow God to energize and direct us. God is still sovereign! God is still on His throne! Christ has won the victory and will reveal His triumph, He is King of Kings and Lord of Lords! Christ still saves and keeps! He has not changed and never will. Bless His Holy Name.

God bless you as you labor for Him.

Jimmy Draper

James T. Draper, Jr.
President
The Sunday School Board

Fresh Encounter

A Heart Cry for Revival • From across the nation and around the world, an intensifying cry is being raised to God for a fresh encounter with Him in revival. Almost everywhere we go we hear churches cry out for revival. They are saying that what they are experiencing is so inferior, so dry, and so empty they want a fresh touch from God. They want to experience God in the ways God's people experienced His mighty power and presence in the Scriptures and in history. But, many are saying, "We don't know what to do." Their heart cry is: "Is there a word from the Lord? What does God say we need to do?" We are convinced that God hears such a cry.

These materials have been prayerfully prepared to help you and your church experience genuine revival. Revival is a gracious act of Sovereign God. He desires to give revival far more than you want to receive it. The way to revival is open, and God is extending the invitation for you and your church to return to Him. He is awaiting your response.

Fresh Encounter assists and guides churches to help members develop a sense of corporate identity with accountability and responsibility before God. This process guides churches to examine themselves by God's Word, return to a right relationship with Him, and be filled once again with His presence and power. Two parts make up this process: Understanding God's Pattern and Returning to God.

PART 1: Understanding God's Pattern • The first part of the process involves a six-week study of *God's Pattern for Revival and Spiritual Awakening*. This small-group study process helps members become aware of God's pattern in Scripture and His requirements for revival. It also helps churches reestablish a corporate identity before God as His people. This study can be preceded by viewing the video messages on *Introduction to Fresh Encounter* which overview God's pattern for revival and spiritual awakening.

PART 2: Returning to God • The second part of the process guides churches in times of corporate worship using *A Plumb Line for God's People*. God's Word serves as a plumb line to reveal God's ideal for the body of Christ (the church) and for Christian living. Six video messages focus on some of the most common areas in which God's people depart from Him. When individuals or churches recognize that they have departed, they immediately need to repent and return to a right love relationship with God. These messages include:

- God's Standard for the Family
- Religion vs. Reality
- Substitutes for God
- World's Ways vs. Kingdom Ways
- Unholy Living vs. Holy Living
- Broken Relationships vs. Unity in the Body

These six messages are not sequential. A church can begin with the subject area they realize needs to be addressed first. Time should then be allotted for the corporate body to process what God is saying and respond by doing whatever He requires. Individuals and churches should stay with one subject before God as long as necessary for God to restore them to a right relationship with Him. The Leader's Manual provides guidance for the use of these messages.

Contents

Invitation to FRESH ENCOUNTER

1. God Is at Work • Many Christians and churches seem to be in great despair over the spiritual and moral condition of our nation and our churches. Conditions are desperate. Don't be discouraged, however. Rejoice! Never have I seen a deeper or more profound hunger among the people of God for a spiritual revival than I see right now. God is at work stirring the hearts of His people to pray and seek His face.

Every mighty movement of God has been preceded by terrible conditions, a heart cry for revival, and a sweeping movement in united, concerted, extraordinary prayer. Without a doubt, that is the order of the day. Leaders across the nation and in various groups and denominations believe we are in the midst of the greatest movement of prayer ever in human history. Nothing has ever equaled what is happening now in united prayer worldwide, in national and international networks of prayer in cities, among pastors, in churches, on college campuses, in homes, and in individual lives. When God finally gets His people to pray like this, revival is on the way.

2. God's Ideal: A Love Relationship • God created you (as an individual and as a church) for an intimate and personal love relationship with Him. Jesus said the most important commandment of God is this:

"Hear, O Israel, the Lord our God, the Lord is one. Love the Lord your God with all your heart and with all your soul and with all your mind and with all your strength."
—Mark 12:29,30

More than anything, God wants you to love Him. This is God's ideal for your life—a love relationship with Him. Those who have placed their faith in Jesus Christ's saving grace and have surrendered their lives fully to Him as Lord have new life in Him. Jesus said, "This is eternal life: that they may know you, the only true God, and Jesus Christ, whom you have sent" (John 17:3). You come to know God when you experience the love relationship with Him for which you were created.

Notice that the greatest commandment in Mark 12:30 is addressed to God's people, not to individuals. The full dimension of God's love is experienced within the context of God's people. God has fashioned His people into a living body of Christ—the church. A church is a people in meaningful, personal relationship with Jesus Christ and one another. These people enter into this relationship with one another and then watch to see how God will thrust them into His world redemptive plan. God's ideal is for His people to love Him with their total being. In that love relationship, God will reveal Himself and His mighty power. In a love relationship with God, God's people will have a similar quality of love for one another revealing to the world that they are Jesus' disciples. (See 1 John 1:7 and John 13:34-35.)

3. Sin Brings Discipline • Even if you have a love relationship with God, you and your church will tend to depart from that relationship because of sin. Individuals break the intimate fellowship with God. Churches also can sin, breaking fellowship with God. But God is love. God continues to love His people even when they rebel against His lordship—His rule—over them.

When you move out of fellowship and away from the love relationship with God, He disciplines you. Because of His holiness and His justice, God must punish sin and rebellion. God disciplines individuals, families, and churches so they will come back to the love relationship that brings abundant life.

"My son, do not make light of the Lord's discipline, and do not lose heart when he rebukes you, because the Lord disciplines those he loves, and he punishes everyone he accepts as a son"

—*Hebrews 12:5-6*

God disciplines His children out of His love for them. God knows that the best life possible is found only in an intimate love relationship with Him. God's rebuke or discipline is His invitation to return to Him. Are you experiencing the discipline of the Lord? Is your church experiencing the rebuke or punishment of God? God disciplines only those He loves. Discipline is God's invitation for you to return to Him.

4. God's Invitation: Return to Your First Love • In the first letter to the churches in Revelation, the risen Christ extended an invitation to which most of us need to respond. The letter was to the church in Ephesus. Jesus commended their hard work, their perseverance, and their intolerance of evil. Yet they had a fatal flaw.

"Yet I hold this against you: You have forsaken your first love. Remember the height from which you have fallen! Repent and do the things you did at first. If you do not repent, I will come to you and remove your lampstand from its place. To him who overcomes, I will give the right to eat from the tree of life, which is in the paradise of God."

—*Revelation 2:4-5,7*

The primary reason we need revival is that we have forsaken our love relationship with God—our first love. God's invitation is for us to realize that we have fallen and to repent and return to our first love. His word to the church at Ephesus indicates that failure to repent is fatal. He said he would remove their lampstand if they refused to return to their first love for Him. To the extent that we fail to

return to our first love, we will miss out on the abundant life He intends for His people, and the world will fail to know God's redeeming love.

5. God's Plumb Line • In Scripture God uses the idea of a plumb line to describe what He is doing with His people (see Amos 7:7-8). God built His people like a straight wall—true to plumb. When we depart from Him, one of our problems is that we do not realize how far we have departed. We often don't understand how seriously we have strayed from Him. We may not realize how close we are to complete collapse or destruction. God holds a plumb line beside His people so they can see how far they have departed.

The Leaning Tower of Pisa is a physical example of our problem. A bell tower was built in Pisa, Italy. The tower is 177 feet tall and made from solid marble. The ground beneath the tower was not solid enough to support the weight of the tower, and it began to sink on one side. Now the tower leans more than 17 feet off center. The walls are straight, but the whole building is leaning. The problem is with the foundation. If the foundation were firm and in line, the walls would be in line as well. If a huge crane could pull the walls to plumb again, the problem would still exist. Without a solid foundation the tower would fall right back to its crooked state.

In a similar way your spiritual life has its foundation in a love relationship with God. The way you live your life, practice your faith, and obey God's commands can be represented by the tower. That your life or your church is out of line with God's plan is only the visible symptom of a root problem. The problem is in your love relationship. Jesus said, "He who does not love me will not obey my teaching" (John 14:24) but "if anyone loves me, he will obey my teaching" (John 14:23).

God's Word reveals God Himself, His purposes, and His ways. The Scriptures serve as His plumb line for us. When we can see we have departed from God's ideals, purposes, ways, and commands, we can know clearly that we have left our love relationship with Him. You cannot love God appropriately and disobey Him. It is spiritually impossible. If you are not obeying Him, it is because you do not love Him as you should.

6. Revival • Genuine revival does not come simply by reforming your behavior. Just changing your ways is not sufficient. Unless your love relationship with God is repaired, you will eventually go back to your old ways of living. The only lasting motivation for obedience to God is a firm love relationship with Him. If your love relationship with God is right, your life will line up with His standards. This is a matter of the heart.

Do you see the connection? A right love relationship with God is the requirement for genuine revival. Correct behavior comes because of the love relationship. To change behavior without a change in the relationship with God is only temporary and superficial. Revival requires a change of heart.

Revival means to restore or renew life. Revival is for God's people who need a fresh encounter, a fresh love relationship with Him. Revival is God's putting the plumb line of His Word right down the middle of His people. God calls us to repent and return to a holy love relationship with Him. When we repent and return to Him, God turns our hearts back to Himself. He forgives. He cleanses. He restores life—God's life to His people. This is revival. God gives renewed life. God is our life.

When your love relationship is right, your obedience and faithfulness will follow. Jesus said, "If you love me, you will obey what I command" (John 14:15). Repentance and revival are not just a reform of behavior. Revival has not taken place unless a change of character and a change of heart have taken place. When your love for the Lord compels you to obey Him and you have put away everything that offends God, revival has occurred.

7. Spiritual Awakening • When people turn to Christ for salvation in large numbers, spiritual awakening is taking place. Spiritual awakening of the lost to saving faith in Christ is a by-product of the revival of God's people. During the following six weeks, we will examine seven phases in God's pattern for revival and spiritual awakening. They are described on page 99 of this book.

God has a plan to redeem the world. God has chosen a people through whom He will work to carry out that plan. When God's people sin and leave their right relationship with Him, He disciplines them to bring them back to Him. When we cry out to God and repent, He revives His people, exalts His Son Jesus, and brings healing in the land. Here is the promise of God for revival of His people and spiritual awakening in the land:

"When I shut up the heavens so that there is no rain, or command locusts to devour the land or send a plague among my people, if my people, who are called by my name, will humble themselves and pray and seek my face and turn from their wicked ways, then will I hear from heaven and will forgive their sin and will heal their land."
— 2 Chronicles 7:13-14

Dear brothers and sisters in Christ:
For the sake of God's glory, because of His love, to honor His Son Jesus in His body—the church, for the sake of our children and relatives, for the sake of our neighbors and friends, for the healing of our nation . . .
Let us, as God's chosen people:
• humble ourselves
• pray
• cry out to God and seek His face
• turn from our wicked ways
• and fall deeply in love with Jesus again!

WARNING!

The purpose of *Fresh Encounter* is to guide you and your church to stand before God in a fresh encounter with Him. You can anticipate that God is going to be speaking to His church during this study. The Holy Spirit has the assignment to reveal truth and to convict of sin, righteousness, and judgment. Whenever God speaks, He calls for obedience. Do you want God to speak to you? Then you must be prepared to obey Him when He does. To hear the Creator of the universe speak to you and then refuse to obey is a terrible offense to God. He is your Creator. God has every right to be Lord of your life.

Do not start this study unless you mean business with God. If the Holy Spirit takes the Word of God and brings you face-to-face with God, you are accountable for the relationship. At that point you either must reject Him or obey Him. To sin in ignorance is one thing, but God judges much more severely those who sin with knowledge of the truth (see 2 Pet. 2:20-21). Jesus asked His followers this penetrating question: "Why do you call me, 'Lord, Lord,' and do not do what I say?" (Luke 6:46).

You will not be able to go through this material without coming to know what God requires for His people to return to Him and become His instruments to reach a lost world. If you work through this study and decide not to obey God, you will be worse off than before. You will be better off not to take this course than to take it and say no to God's will. You cannot encounter God and say no without becoming hardened in heart.

Once you recognize the seriousness of this study, ask God what it will cost your church if you do not go through a process of repentance.

SOME POSSIBLE RESPONSES • Not everyone will respond positively to these materials. Scripture is our guide to know how God relates to His people. Scripture also reveals sinfulness and rebelliousness. Here are some responses you may observe from people who study these materials with you.

- Some may discount the truth from the Old Testament saying, "God is not like that anymore." God, however, does not change. God of the Old Testament is the same God of the New Testament. The Scriptures from Genesis to Revelation reveal Him and the ways He relates to His people. God says, "I the Lord do not change" (Mal. 3:6). James 1:17 says that the "Father of the heavenly lights [the Creator] does not change."

- Some are offended to think of God as a God of judgment. They choose to focus only on God's love and mercy. They try to exert "positive thinking" hoping to bring about a positive result. In Scripture God condemned those who went about saying, "Peace, peace" when there was no peace (Jer. 6:14). In the middle of a sinful church, some will say, "We are a great church. Nothing is wrong." God said through Jeremiah, "The prophet who prophesies peace will be recognized as one truly sent by the Lord only if his prediction comes true" (Jer. 28:9). You can use the same criteria.

- Some will refuse to deal openly with sin in the church (past sins as well as present ones). To protect the church's or a person's reputation some may disobey the clear teaching of God on how to deal with the issue. They prefer to "forget about the past" and move forward. To harbor or refuse to deal with open sin in God's way is a sure way to shut down God's activity in a church. If we regard iniquity in our heart, God refuses to even hear our prayers (see Ps. 66:18). Such a light treatment of sin can lead to open rebellion on the part of many. Sin can spread like a fast growing cancer if not thoroughly dealt with in repentance. Sometimes God requires that sin be dealt with openly in a congregation. To cover up such sins is corporate rebellion on the part of a church.

- Some will choose to rely on human wisdom and reason even when it is in direct opposition to God's Word. They may be very vocal and forceful. They may present their case in such a way that they say, "Anyone who disagrees with me is a fool." They may argue against God's ways even when confronted with a clear word from Scripture.

11

Do not allow such people to stand in the way of you or your church's following what God says in His Word.

STUDY TIPS FOR GOD'S PATTERN

God's Pattern for Revival and Spiritual Awakening is a personal guide to understanding how God works with His people to bring them back to a right relationship with Him through revival. Use the following suggestions to get the most out of your study.

Individual Study • As you probably have noticed, this is a workbook for individual study. The lessons guide you through a study of the Scriptures to understand God's pattern for revival and spiritual awakening.

These materials have been designed for use in the body of Christ. Though individual study is helpful, you will miss much of what God may have in store for you if you fail to participate with others. If you are not in a group already, consider getting together with Christian friends for the study.

1. Read the Unit Pages. They will give you an overview of each unit with important summary statements.
2. Memorize Scripture. Each week you will be given one Scripture to memorize. Allow God's Word to be a lamp to your feet and a light to your path (see Ps. 119:105). Hide His Word in your heart and mind so that you will not sin against Him (see Ps. 119:11). Six Scriptures are on page 100 of this book so that you can review them daily.
3. Receive Inspiration from Revival Accounts. Let the testimony of God's mighty activity in past revivals inspire you to desire a fresh encounter with God in your family, church, denomination, city, or nation. Consider reading more about these revivals in the books listed.
4. Experience Cleansing and Filling through the Word. Each unit has a list of Scriptures in "Cleansing by Washing with Water Through the Word." Pray through each Scripture and let God work in you to cleanse things in your life that are not best. Let Him fill you

with wisdom, knowledge, virtue, and instruction. Reading the Scriptures in the presence of the Holy Spirit is an encounter with God that will change you.

5. Complete Daily Lessons. Each unit has five daily lessons. Most lessons should take no more than 15 minutes. Take time to complete each activity.
6. Encounter God in Prayer. At the end of each lesson are instructions for "Encountering God in Prayer." Look on these as opportunities to spend time in fellowship with your Heavenly Father. You may want to set aside longer periods on some days to allow for plenty of time for God to speak with you. Don't get in a hurry. These times may be the fresh encounters with Him that you long for. Consider keeping a journal to record prayers and God's responses.
7. Review the Unit. Complete the review at the end of each unit. If you need help with any of the questions, look back through the unit for the answers. Pay special attention to what God may have said to you during the unit of study.

Group Study • Helps for this study are in *Fresh Encounter Leader's Manual*. These resources can be used by churches or groups in a variety of settings including: (1) In preparation for and during scheduled "revival" services; (2) Sunday mornings during a study time and in congregational worship; (3) Sunday evenings during a study time and in congregational worship; (4) At other study and response times during the week; (5) During an extended period of examination on a day (or weekend) of prayer and fasting.

Unit 1: An Overview of God's Pattern

"Revival" and "spiritual awakening" are two different experiences. In this first unit you will come to understand what we mean by "revival" and "spiritual awakening" and study an example of each one from the Bible. In Day 4 you will be introduced to seven phases in God's pattern for revival and spiritual awakening.

DAY 1: SPIRITUAL AWAKENING AND REVIVAL

DAY 2: SPIRITUAL AWAKENING ON PENTECOST

DAY 3: A CYCLE OF SIN AND REVIVAL

DAY 4: SEVEN PHASES IN GOD'S PATTERN

DAY 5: REVIVAL UNDER EZRA AND NEHEMIAH

LEARNING GOAL

You will understand the difference between revival and spiritual awakening and know the seven phases in God's pattern for revival and spiritual awakening. You will express your willingness to obey God as He reveals His will during this study.

SCRIPTURE MEMORY VERSE

2 Chronicles 7:14
"If my people, who are called by my name, will humble themselves and pray and seek my face and turn from their wicked ways, then will I hear from heaven and will forgive their sin and will heal their land."

SUMMARY STATEMENTS

- Spiritual awakening is when large numbers of people (or a large percentage of people in an area) experience new birth to spiritual life in a short period of time.
- Revival is a return to spiritual health after a period of decline into sin and broken fellowship with God.
- Revival is for God's people when they need to be forgiven and restored to life, spiritual health, and vitality.
- Revival is God's restoring spiritual health and vitality to His people.
- When God's people surrender themselves fully to the work of the Holy Spirit, God will draw a watching world to Himself.
- On the Day of Pentecost the church began with 120 believers and God added 3,000 in a single day. That is spiritual awakening!
- As the people of God maintain a right relationship with Him, it is reflected in their love for one another.
- When God's people depart from a right relationship with Him, they need revival.
- The joy of His presence and genuine worship strengthen God's people for the work of repentance to follow.
- Worship alone cannot bring about revival. God requires repentance.

Spiritual Awakening in Wales

In the fall of 1904 a revival broke out in Wales. During the next six months, 100,000 people were saved in a great spiritual awakening. No one organized the campaign. They did not use advertising, public relations, radio broadcasts, or great soul winning and witnessing campaigns. God did a sovereign work that captured the attention of the world. When the Spirit of God fell on a people who were right with Him, things began to happen. Without anybody witnessing to them, people cried out: "What must I do to be saved?"

Wales is a principality of Great Britain west of London. The area has a wonderful history of revivals among God's people. By the beginning of this century people had a longing for a fresh wind of God's Spirit. The last great revival had taken place in 1859-60. Church membership had declined. People were indifferent to religious matters. The churches were formal. God's people needed revival.

By 1904 God was at work in many places and in many people throughout Wales. The nation was like a tinder box God had prepared for the quick spread of revival fires. God chose to use a young boy named Evan Roberts in a special way. Evan worked in the coal mines of Wales, but he had a great burden for revival. For 13 years he prayed for an outpouring of God's Spirit. Prayer meetings with different groups of God's people became a major emphasis in his life. Early in 1904 Evan accepted God's call to preach, and he went to school to prepare.

Following a Sunday School service, Seth Joshua led in prayer. One of his requests was, "Lord, bend us." The Spirit of God used that simple statement to touch Evan's heart. On his way out the door he kept praying, "O Lord, bend me!"

God gave Evan a burden to go to his home church in Loughor to conduct a week of services with the young people. Following a Monday night prayer meeting on October 31, 1904, seventeen young people stayed to hear Evan's message. His message had four points:

1. YOU MUST PUT AWAY ANY UNCONFESSED SIN.
2. YOU MUST PUT AWAY ANY DOUBTFUL HABIT.
3. YOU MUST OBEY THE SPIRIT PROMPTLY.
4. YOU MUST CONFESS CHRIST PUBLICLY.

That night all seventeen responded to his appeal. Crowds increased nightly. The Spirit was poured out on the nation as God's people returned to Him. Lost people were dramatically converted—70,000 in two months, 85,000 in five months, and over 100,000 in the six months following that October meeting.

These commitments were life changing. Taverns closed due to the lack of business. The crime rate dropped radically leaving the police with little to do. People paid old debts and made restitution for thefts and other wrongs committed. There was even a work slowdown in the coal mines as the mules had to learn the new language of the converted miners.

News of the revival spread to other countries, and people were stirred to prayer. Soon God was at work in nations around the world bringing people to Himself.

◆ **Read the four points of Evan Roberts' message and ask God if He wants you to respond to Him in any specific area of your life.**

For further reading on the Wales Awakening see: *The Flaming Tongue* by J. Edwin Orr, Chicago: Moody Press, 1973; or *Glory Filled the Land* edited by Richard Owen Roberts, Wheaton: International Awakening Press, 1989.

Cleansing by Washing with Water Through the Word

> *Christ loved the church and gave himself up for her to make her holy, cleansing her by the washing with water through the word, and to present her to himself as a radiant church, without stain or wrinkle or any other blemish, but holy and blameless.*
> —Ephesians 5:25-27

Read and pray through the following Scriptures this week. Let God speak to you through His Word. Draw arrows in the margins to mark passages.

WASH OUT: Are there actions, behaviors, habits, or sins that need to be "washed out" of your life? your family? your church? Confess them (agree with God about the wrong) and turn away from them and to God.

WASH IN: Are there good things God wants to "wash into" your life? your family? your church? Pray about those and become all God wants you to be.

2 PETER 1:3-9 • ³His divine power has given us everything we need for life and godliness through our knowledge of him who called us by his own glory and goodness. ⁴Through these he has given us his very great and precious promises, so that through them you may participate in the divine nature and escape the corruption in the world caused by evil desires.

⁵For this very reason, make every effort to add to your faith goodness; and to goodness, knowledge; ⁶and to knowledge, self-control; and to self-control, perseverance; and to perseverance, godliness; ⁷and to godliness, brotherly kindness; and to brotherly kindness, love. ⁸For if you possess these qualities in increasing measure, they will keep you from being ineffective and unproductive in your knowledge of our Lord Jesus Christ. ⁹But if anyone does not have them, he is nearsighted and blind, and has forgotten that he has been cleansed from his past sins.

PHILIPPIANS 4:8 • Finally, brothers, whatever is true, whatever is noble, whatever is right, whatever is pure, whatever is lovely, whatever is admirable—if anything is excellent or praiseworthy—think about such things.

PSALM 24:3-5 • ³Who may ascend the hill of the Lord? Who may stand in his holy place? ⁴He who has clean hands and a pure heart, who does not lift up his soul to an idol or swear by what is false. ⁵He will receive blessing from the Lord.

PSALM 15:1-5 • ¹Lord, who may dwell in your sanctuary? Who may live on your holy hill? ²He whose walk is blameless and who does what is righteous, who speaks the truth from his heart ³and has no slander on his tongue, who does his neighbor no wrong and casts no slur on his fellowman, ⁴who despises a vile man but honors those who fear the Lord, who keeps his oath even when it hurts, ⁵who lends his money without usury and does not accept a bribe against the innocent. He who does these things will never be shaken.

TITUS 2:11-14 • ¹¹The grace of God that brings salvation has appeared to all men. ¹²It teaches us to say "No" to ungodliness and worldly passions, and to live self-controlled, upright and godly lives in this present age, ¹³while we wait for the blessed hope—the glorious appearing of our great God and Savior, Jesus Christ, ¹⁴who gave himself for us to redeem us from all wickedness and to purify for himself a people that are his very own, eager to do what is good.

Day 1: Spiritual Awakening and Revival

SPIRITUAL AWAKENING • Spiritual awakening is large numbers of people (or a large percentage of people in an area) experiencing new birth to spiritual life in a short period of time. Spiritual awakenings are not just times of mass decisions for Christ. Decisions may or may not reflect a new birth. In a spiritual awakening people's lives are changed radically (see 2 Cor. 5:17). Often the result of a spiritual awakening is a changed society in a city or a nation. Major social reforms often have accompanied spiritual awakening as people put off the old life of sin and put on the new life in Christ.

♦ Define "spiritual awakening" in your own words.

Spiritual awakening is _____

_____

_____

_____

REVIVAL • The word revival has a variety of meanings for Christians. For some it means a series of meetings in the spring or fall. Some think of revival as a time when people place their faith in Christ and receive Him as Savior and Lord. Other people have used the term revival to describe a spiritual awakening.

JOHN 3:6,16-18,36 • [6]Flesh gives birth to flesh, but the Spirit gives birth to spirit. [16]God so loved the world that he gave his one and only Son, that whoever believes in him shall not perish but have eternal life. [17]For God did not send his Son into the world to condemn the world, but to save the world through him. [18]Whoever believes in him is not condemned, but whoever does not believe stands condemned already because he has not believed in the name of God's one and only Son. [36]Whoever believes in the Son has eternal life, but whoever rejects the Son will not see life, for God's wrath remains on him.

2 CORINTHIANS 5:17 • If anyone is in Christ, he is a new creation; the old has gone, the new has come!

WHAT IS GENUINE REVIVAL? The root word revive is made up of two parts: *re* meaning "again" and *vive* meaning "to live." Thus, revive means "to live again, to come or be brought back to life, health, or vitality." Revival is a time when spiritual life and vitality are restored. Revival is a return to spiritual health after a period of spiritual decline into sin and broken fellowship with God. We will use the word revival to describe what God does to restore His people to a right relationship with Him. Revival is for God's people when they need to be forgiven and restored to life, spiritual health, and vitality.

♦ Write the words *revival* and *spiritual awakening* beside their descriptions:

_____ is a large percentage of people accepting Jesus Christ as Savior and Lord.

_____ _____ ___ is God restoring spiritual health and vitality to His people.

Spiritual awakening is a large percentage of people turning to Jesus as Savior and Lord. A *revival* is for God's people when they have declined spiritually because of sin. When God's people return to Him and God restores them to a right relationship with Himself, revival has taken place.

GOD'S PROMISE FOR REVIVAL

If my people, who are called by my name, will humble themselves and pray and seek my face and turn from their wicked ways, then will I hear from heaven and will forgive their sin and will heal their land.
—*2 Chronicles 7:14*

♦ 2 Chronicles 7:14 describes God's promise for revival. Complete the activity below and begin to memorize God's promise for revival.

♦ Read 2 Chronicles 7:14 (above) and answer the questions below about God's promise for revival.

What four things does God require of His people before He will revive them?
a. _____ themselves
b. _____
c. seek _____
d. turn from _____ _____

When God's people meet His requirements, what does He promise to do?
a. _____ from heaven
b. _____ _____ their sin
c. _____ their land

Day 2: Spiritual Awakening on Pentecost

When Jesus was arrested, tried, and crucified, the disciples deserted Him. Peter with curses even denied knowing Jesus. In a sense, the days between His resurrection and His return to heaven provided time for renewal of the disciples' relationship with Jesus. These days also provided time for Jesus to further prepare them with teachings about the Kingdom (see Acts 1:3). He explained all that the Scriptures had to say about Himself (Luke 24:27).

When the Holy Spirit came on the Day of Pentecost, He empowered the early church for the first time. At this point the church did not need revival (renewal of life). As a newly empowered church, they were just beginning to experience the fullness of life God intended for His people.

♦ Read Acts 2:1-2,4-8,11-12.
1. Underline in verse 4 what happened to the believers that brought about a change in their experience of life.
2. In verses 4 and 6 circle the words that describe the miracle that occurred in their lives.
3. Underline in verse 11 the subject the believers declared to the crowds in Jerusalem.

SPIRITUAL AWAKENING • When God's people surrender themselves fully to the work of the Holy Spirit, God will draw a watching world to Himself. Peter answered the questions of the crowd by preaching from the Old Testament Scriptures about the coming of the Holy Spirit. He then proclaimed Jesus the Christ. The message was brief; but, since God was working through him, the results had God-sized dimensions.

LUKE 24:27 • Beginning with Moses and all the Prophets, he explained to them what was said in all the Scriptures concerning himself.

ACTS 2:1-2,4-8,11-12 • ¹When the day of Pentecost came, they were all together in one place. ²Suddenly a sound like the blowing of a violent wind came from heaven and filled the whole house where they were sitting.

⁴All of them were filled with the Holy Spirit and began to speak in other tongues as the Spirit enabled them.

⁵Now there were staying in Jerusalem God-fearing Jews from every nation under heaven. ⁶When they heard this sound, a crowd came together in bewilderment, because each one heard them speaking in his own language. ⁷Utterly amazed, they asked: "Are not all these men who are speaking Galileans? ⁸Then how is it that each of us hears them in his own native language?

¹¹we hear them declaring the wonders of God in our own tongues!" ¹²Amazed and perplexed, they asked one another, "What does this mean?"

◆ Read the conclusion of Peter's message in Acts 2:36-38,41 and write the number of people who accepted his message. _____

This is the purest example we have in Scripture of what God will do in spiritual awakening when He has a people rightly related and fully surrendered to Him. God displayed His powers through the believers as they spoke foreign languages they had not learned. After only a brief message, people "were cut to the heart." Three thousand accepted the message, repented, were baptized, and received the gift of the Holy Spirit. The church began with 120 believers, and God added 3,000 in a single day. That is spiritual awakening!

◆ Read Acts 2:42-47 and circle words that describe the "life" experienced by the believers.

The people in the early church were filled with awe. Their lives were changed. They lived unselfishly with glad and sincere hearts. They praised God and enjoyed the favor of all the people. Wouldn't you like to be part of a church like that? As the people of God maintained a right relationship with Him, it was reflected in their love for one another. God used that demonstration of God-like love among human beings as a real attraction to the lost people of Jerusalem, and spiritual awakening continued!

ACTS 2:36-38,41 • 36"Therefore let all Israel be assured of this: God has made this Jesus, whom you crucified, both Lord and Christ."
37When the people heard this, they were cut to the heart and said to Peter and the other apostles, "Brothers, what shall we do?"
38Peter replied, "Repent and be baptized, every one of you, in the name of Jesus Christ for the forgiveness of your sins. And you will receive the gift of the Holy Spirit."
41Those who accepted his message were baptized, and about three thousand were added to their number that day.

ACTS 2:42-47 • 42They devoted themselves to the apostles' teaching and to the fellowship, to the breaking of bread and to prayer. 43Everyone was filled with awe, and many wonders and miraculous signs were done by the apostles. 44All the believers were together and had everything in common. 45Selling their possessions and goods, they gave to anyone as he had need. 46Every day they continued to meet together in the temple courts. They broke bread in their homes and ate together with glad and sincere hearts, 47praising God and enjoying the favor of all the people. And the Lord added to their number daily those who were being saved.

ENCOUNTERING GOD IN PRAYER
Pray about your church. Ask God what changes need to take place in your church for it to be used in the spiritual awakening of your community. As God reveals insights, write them in the margins.

Day 3: A Cycle of Sin and Revival

Yesterday you studied the account of a spiritual awakening on the Day of Pentecost. God had a people rightly related to Himself, so God was able to display His glory to a watching world. God exalted His Son Jesus through His people and drew the lost to saving faith in Christ. The early church is the example of what God intends for the church to be. Churches, however, don't always stay in right relationship with God. They tend to depart from Him. When God's people have departed from a right relationship with Him, they need revival.

A CYCLE IN THE BOOK OF JUDGES • The cycle described above is a problem that God's people have always had.

♦ Read the verses at the right from Judges 2 that give an example of the cycle God's people went through repeatedly.

Now, following the cycle, number the items below in the correct order from 1 (first) through 5 (last).
_____a. God brought judgment on the people and allowed them to suffer defeat by their enemies.
_____b. God raised up a deliverer and restored the people to a right relationship with Himself.
_____c. The people loved the Lord and served Him.
_____d. The people cried out to the Lord for help.
_____e. The people departed from the Lord and served other gods.

In the Book of Judges we see this cycle repeated over and over again. This cycle is seen frequently in the Old Testament. (Answers: a-3; b-5; c-1; d-4; e-2.)

JUDGES 2

1. The People Served the Lord
⁷The people served the Lord throughout the lifetime of Joshua and of the elders who outlived him and who had seen all the great things the Lord had done for Israel.

2. The People Forsook the Lord
¹¹Then the Israelites did evil in the eyes of the Lord and served the Baals. ¹²They forsook the Lord, the God of their fathers.

3. God Defeated Them Through Enemies
¹⁴In his anger against Israel the Lord handed them over to raiders who plundered them. He sold them to their enemies. ¹⁵Whenever Israel went out to fight, the hand of the Lord was against them to defeat them.

4. The People Cried Out for Help
¹⁵They were in great distress. ¹⁸They groaned under those who oppressed and afflicted them.

5. God Had Compassion and Delivered
¹⁶The Lord raised up judges, who saved them out of the hands of these raiders. ¹⁸The Lord had compassion on them.

♦ Read the summary of the next cycle in Judges 3:7-11.

NEW TESTAMENT CHURCHES • This problem is not just an Old Testament problem for Israel. The problem of departing from a right relationship with God is a problem for New Testament churches as well. In Revelation 2–3 we read the words of the resurrected Christ as he calls different churches to repent and return to Him.

♦ Read the verses at the right from Revelation 2 and 3 and circle the word *repent* every time it occurs. Do you believe that churches in our day depart from God so that they need to repent and return to Him? ❑ Yes ❑ No

This cycle of departure and return to the Lord is characteristic of God's people throughout the ages. The way God deals with His people in this cycle forms a pattern. This book is a study of that pattern in the Scriptures. It is more than a study of the history of Israel or a history of the church. It is a study of God and how He works with His people to accomplish His mission to bring a world to Himself.

♦ Your Scripture Memory Verse summarizes God's promise for revival. Review 2 Chronicles 7:14 on page 100 of this book. Continue to review it this week.

JUDGES 3:7-11 • [7]The Israelites did evil in the eyes of the Lord; they forgot the Lord their God. [8]The anger of the Lord burned against Israel so that he sold them into the hands of [the king of Aram] . . . to whom the Israelites were subject for eight years. [9]But when they cried out to the Lord, he raised up for them a deliverer, Othniel. [10]The Spirit of the Lord came upon him. . . . The Lord gave . . . [the] king of Aram into the hands of Othniel, who overpowered him. [11]So the land had peace for forty years.

REVELATION 2–3

To the church at Ephesus: "You have forsaken your first love. Repent and do the things you did at first" (Rev. 2:4-5).

To the church at Pergamum: "I have a few things against you. Repent therefore!" (Rev. 2:14,16).

To the church at Sardis: "I know your deeds; you have a reputation of being alive, but you are dead. Remember, therefore, what you have received and heard; obey it, and repent" (Rev. 3:1,3).

To the church at Laodicea: "I know your deeds, that you are neither cold nor hot. You are lukewarm. Those whom I love I rebuke and discipline. So be earnest, and repent" (Rev. 3:15,16,19).

ENCOUNTERING GOD IN PRAYER

Ask God to begin to open your spiritual eyes to see what He is doing in and around your life. Ask Him for wisdom and understanding about you, your family's, and your church's relationship to Him.

Day 4: Seven Phases in God's Pattern

♦ Turn to page 99 of this book so that you can look at the diagram of "God's Pattern for Revival and Spiritual Awakening."

The remainder of this book will help you understand how God works with His people to bring them to experience fullness of life. The diagram you see on page 99 helps to illustrate the pattern we see in Scripture. Each of the following units will study one or more phases in this cycle. Let's take a quick look at the seven phases in God's pattern for revival and spiritual awakening.

♦ Read the seven phases in God's pattern below. Circle a key word or phrase in each that might help you remember the main subject. Then write the words/phrases on the lines at the right.

PHASE 1: **God is on mission to redeem a lost world. God calls His people into a relationship with Himself, and He accomplishes His work through them.**
God has called the church to be His people. God wants to work through them to proclaim Christ and bring lost men, women, and children to faith in Him.

PHASE 2: **God's people tend to depart from Him, turning to substitutes for His presence, purposes, and ways.**
God knows that His people can experience fullness of life in a right relationship with Him.

PHASE 3: **God disciplines His people out of His love for them.**
Because of God's love, He disciplines wayward Christians and churches to bring them back to Himself.

1. On Mission

2. _____

3. _____

4. _____

5. _____

6. _____

7. _____

PHASE 4: **God's people cry out to Him for help.**
God's discipline becomes more and more intense until His people cry out to Him. He is patient and long-suffering. Like the Father of the prodigal son, God waits eagerly for His children to return to Him.

PHASE 5: **God calls His people to repent and return to Him or perish.**
God clearly defines the requirements for repentance. He doesn't give options. Churches can return to Him or suffer the consequences of their sin.

PHASE 6: **God revives His repentant people by restoring them to a right relationship with Himself.**
God stands ready to receive His people when they return. He cleanses and forgives. He gives a new heart to serve Him and fullness of the Holy Spirit to empower them for His work. He restores the joy of being in the family of God.

PHASE 7: **God exalts His Son Jesus in His people and draws the lost to saving faith in Him.**
When God has a people rightly related to Him, He is able to display His glory to a watching world. When a people experience the mighty power of God bringing wholeness to their lives, others will notice and want a similar experience of life.

THANKSGIVING LIST

_____

_____

_____

_____

_____

_____

_____

_____

_____

ENCOUNTERING GOD IN PRAYER
Reflect on the wonderful things God has done for you like the gift of His Son Jesus, the presence of the Holy Spirit, the joy of your salvation, and the spiritual blessings God has given. Spend time now and throughout this day praising God and worshiping Him. Make a thanksgiving list above.

Day 5: Revival Under Ezra and Nehemiah

During one of the cycles in the Old Testament, God judged Judah by sending them into exile in Babylon. After 70 years, God began to bring the people back to Jerusalem. A significant revival took place under the leadership of Ezra the priest/scribe and Nehemiah the governor.

♦ Read Nehemiah 7:73–8:6.

Israel assembled to hear a word from the Lord. Who attended the assembly?
- ❑ Only those who could work it into their busy schedule
- ❑ Only those who had a real interest in spiritual growth
- ❑ All the people who could understand
- ❑ Only the adult leaders

With which of the following did the revival begin?
- ❑ With weeping, confession, and repentance
- ❑ With praise and worship of the Lord

What do you think is the most unusual fact in this event so far?

Can you imagine being part of a crowd that stood for six hours (daybreak to noon) listening attentively to God's Word being read? Amazing! Another amazing fact from our modern perspective is that *all* the people assembled, all that could understand. This was not an optional event. The people heard how God had called them out as a nation. They heard about all the miracles and mighty acts God had performed for them. They couldn't help but worship Him.

When the people understood the words of the Law, they realized how miserably they and their fathers had failed the Lord. They began to weep and mourn.

NEHEMIAH 7:73–8:1-3,5-6 • [73]When the seventh month came and the Israelites had settled in their towns,

[1]All the people assembled as one man in the square before the Water Gate. They told Ezra the scribe to bring out the Book of the Law of Moses, which the Lord had commanded for Israel.

[2]So on the first day of the seventh month Ezra the priest brought the Law before the assembly, which was made up of men and women and all who were able to understand. [3]He read it aloud from daybreak till noon as he faced the square before the Water Gate in the presence of the men, women and others who could understand. And all the people listened attentively to the Book of the Law.

[5]Ezra opened the book. All the people could see him because he was standing above them; and as he opened it, the people all stood up. [6]Ezra praised the Lord, the great God; and all the people lifted their hands and responded, "Amen! Amen!" Then they bowed down and worshiped the Lord with their faces to the ground.

♦ Read Nehemiah 8:7-10 and underline the words of instruction in verses 9 and 10 that the leaders gave to the people.

The leaders did not want to cut short the worship and praise that was ascending to the Lord. Genuine worship would strengthen them for the work of repentance to follow. The Israelites experienced great joy. Worship alone, however, could not bring about revival. No amount of prayer, feasting, fasting, or Scripture study could. God required repentance. Later that same month, the people assembled for a special time of repentance.

♦ Read Nehemiah 9:1-3 (below right) and circle the words that indicate that the people met God's requirements for revival: humility, prayer (communication with God), seeking His face, and turning from their wicked ways.

The people fasted, wore sackcloth, confessed and turned from their sins, and worshiped the Lord. Following the time of confession, Nehemiah rehearsed all the mighty acts God had performed for His people. He detailed God's judgment on the land because of the sins of the nation. Then Nehemiah guided the people in reaffirming their covenant relationship with God. Revival began and ended with worship.

NEHEMIAH 8:7-10 • [7]The Levites . . . instructed the people in the Law. [8]They read from the Book of the Law of God, making it clear and giving the meaning so that the people could understand what was being read.

[9]Then Nehemiah the governor, Ezra the priest and scribe, and the Levites who were instructing the people said to them all, "This day is sacred to the Lord your God. Do not mourn or weep." For all the people had been weeping as they listened to the words of the Law.

[10]Nehemiah said, "Go and enjoy choice food and sweet drinks, and send some to those who have nothing prepared. This day is sacred to our Lord. Do not grieve, for the joy of the Lord is your strength."

NEHEMIAH 9:1-3 • [1]On the twenty-fourth day of the same month, the Israelites gathered together, fasting and wearing sackcloth and having dust on their heads. [2]Those of Israelite descent had separated themselves from all foreigners. They stood in their places and confessed their sins and the wickedness of their fathers. [3]They stood where they were and read from the Book of the Law of the Lord their God for a quarter of the day, and spent another quarter in confession and in worshiping the Lord their God.

ENCOUNTERING GOD IN PRAYER

The Lord may surface specific requirements for you to experience genuine revival in your life, family, or church. Are you willing to obey whatever God may require? (Consider very carefully.) ❑ yes ❑ no. If you are, tell God. If you are not yet willing to make such a commitment, would you ask God to help you become willing?

Unit 1 Review

♦ As a review of this unit, answer the following questions. If you need help, scan back through the unit for answers.

1. Place an "R" beside the definition of *revival* and "SA" beside the definition for *spiritual awakening*.

____ a. A large number of people, or a large pecentage of people in an area, experiencing new birth to spiritual life in a short period of time.

____ b. A return of God's people to spiritual health after a period of spiritual decline into sin and broken fellowship with God.

2. Give one example from the Bible of each:
   Revival: _____

   Spiritual Awakening: _____

3. What statement, Scripture, or idea has been most meaningful to you in this unit?_____

   _____

   _____

   _____

4. Reword that statement, Scripture, or idea into a prayer response to God._____

   _____

   _____

   _____

   _____

5. Write from memory God's Promise for Revival in 2 Chronicles 7:14.

   _____

   _____

   _____

   _____

   _____

   _____

   _____

6. Based on 2 Chronicles 7:14, what are four requirements for revival?

   1. _____

   2. _____

   3. _____

   4. _____

Unit 2: God Is on Mission in Our World

Since Adam and Eve, people have chosen to sin and experience a broken relationship with God. God is on mission to bring all people back into a right relationship with Him through His Son Jesus. In this unit you will study God's plan to accomplish this reconciliation. You will see how He has chosen to work through people—first Abraham, then Israel, and now the church—to accomplish His work.

DAY 1: PERFECT CREATION AND A BROKEN RELATIONSHIP
DAY 2: GOD PROVIDES REDEMPTION
DAY 3: GOD CHOOSES A PEOPLE
DAY 4: GOD'S ROYAL PRIESTHOOD
DAY 5: GOD'S FELLOW WORKERS

LEARNING GOAL
You will understand God's purpose to redeem a lost world and His plan to work through His people. In your group you will demonstrate your gratitude to God for the privilege of being chosen as His people.

SCRIPTURE MEMORY VERSE
1 Peter 2:9
You are a chosen people, a royal priesthood, a holy nation, a people belonging to God, that you may declare the praises of him who called you out of darkness into his wonderful light.

SUMMARY STATEMENTS
- God's greatest desire for us is that we love Him with all our being.
- This pure and intimate love relationship prepares us for an eternity in His presence.
- Sin causes a broken relationship with God. Because of sin, we are dead.
- The good news of the gospel is that God has provided for our redemption through Jesus Christ.
- The focus of the Scriptures is on God and His activity.
- God chose and called out people who responded to His offer of salvation through faith in His Son.
- God chose His people because of His love.
- Every believer is a priest unto God.
- We are Christ's ambassadors and God's fellow workers.
- Our motivation for this work is the love of Christ—He compels us by His love.
- When God works through us, we will bear much fruit for the Kingdom—fruit that will last.

Shantung Revival

In the 1920's Christian missionaries in North China were grieved over the spiritual condition of the churches. Members showed little or no spiritual sensitivity or concern. The missionaries began to wonder if many people had accepted Christianity mentally but had never been born again.

In 1920, missionaries and Chinese leaders began to devote one day a month to prayer for revival. In March, 1927, the southern revolutionary army burned Nanking, and all missionaries were ordered to Tsingtau or Chefoo for possible evacuation. Those evacuated to Chefoo began to study the Scriptures and ask the Lord why they had been removed from their work. God began to speak through His Word.

MISSIONARIES GET RIGHT WITH GOD • A group of missionaries asked Marie Monsen, an Evangelical Lutheran from Norway, to join their prayer meetings. God began to use her to challenge missionaries and others to get right with God. The missionaries spent days before the Lord. They confessed every known sin. They sought to be reconciled with one another.

During a special prayer time God worked to heal the eyesight of Ola Culpepper. In the middle of their rejoicing, God convicted the missionaries that they were far more concerned about physical healing than they were about the salvation of the Chinese. They once again began to confess sins to the Lord. God was getting a people right with Himself.

THREE QUESTIONS • Marie was again used of the Lord as she asked the missionaries and others three penetrating questions:

1. Have you been born of the Spirit?
2. What evidence do you have of the new birth?
3. Have you been filled with the Holy Spirit?

REVIVAL AND AWAKENING • The hunger for spiritual vitality caused people to do much soul-searching. Christians and especially the leaders were revived and filled with the power of the Holy Spirit. Once Christians were revived, God had clean vessels through which to work. By 1932 revival was spreading.

Many came to realize they were only "head" Christians, but they had never placed their trust in Christ. An evangelist for 25 years, Mr. Chow realized he was trusting in his good works and not Christ for salvation. After he was saved, he refused to be paid for his preaching because he had preached for 25 years without the presence and power of the Lord. Lucy Wright, a missionary nurse for nine years, realized she had only joined the church. She trusted Christ for the first time. In 1932 masses of people were coming to Christ. In one school all 600 girls and 900 out of 1,000 boys trusted Christ during 10 days of meetings. Awakening often follows revival.

RESULTS

- Saved people went everywhere telling everyone what Jesus had done for them. Those who turned to Christ took down their "house gods" and burned them.
- The hearts of God's people were full of praise and thanksgiving. Joyful singing filled the services. New songs were written and the Scripture was put to music.
- All believers had a great hunger for God's Word. Bible classes met nightly, and the Bible schools and seminaries saw significantly increased enrollments.
- Spiritually dead churches were revived. Church attendance multiplied, and the members paid close attention to worship, prayer, and discipleship. Prayer meetings lasted two or three hours as people got right with God and prayed for the lost.
- Broken families and relationships were healed.

This account has been adapted from *Go Home and Tell* by Bertha Smith, Nashville: Broadman Press, 1965, pp. 12-39, and *The Shantung Revival* by C. L. Culpepper, Atlanta, Home Mission Board, 1982.

Cleansing by Washing with Water Through the Word

> *Christ loved the church and gave himself up for her to make her holy, cleansing her by the washing with water through the word, and to present her to himself as a radiant church, without stain or wrinkle or any other blemish, but holy and blameless.*
> —Ephesians 5:25-27

Recall in the Shantung Revival how God worked in the lives of people who professed to be Christians. Read the following Scriptures. Let God speak to you through His Word. Have you been born of the Spirit? What evidence do you have of the new birth?

2 CORINTHIANS 5:17 • If anyone is in Christ, he is a new creation; the old has gone, the new has come!

MATTHEW 7:18-23 • [18]"A good tree cannot bear bad fruit, and a bad tree cannot bear good fruit. [19]Every tree that does not bear good fruit is cut down and thrown into the fire. [20]Thus, by their fruit you will recognize them.
[21] "Not everyone who says to me, 'Lord, Lord' will enter the kingdom of heaven, but only he who does the will of my Father who is in heaven. [22]Many will say to me on that day, 'Lord, Lord, did we not prophesy in your name, and in your name drive out demons and perform many miracles?' [23]Then I will tell them plainly, 'I never knew you. Away from me, you evildoers!'"

GALATIANS 5:22-24 • [22]The fruit of the Spirit is love, joy, peace, patience, kindness, goodness, faithfulness, [23]gentleness and self-control. [24]Those who belong to Christ Jesus have crucified the sinful nature with its passions and desires.

GALATIANS 5:19-21 • [19]The acts of the sinful nature are obvious: sexual immorality, impurity and debauchery; [20]idolatry and witchcraft; hatred, discord, jealousy, fits of rage, selfish ambition, dissensions, factions [21]and envy; drunkenness, orgies, and the like. I warn you, as I did before, that those who live like this will not inherit the kingdom of God.

ROMANS 8:5,7-10 • [5]Those who live according to the sinful nature have their minds set on what that nature desires; but those who live in accordance with the Spirit have their minds set on what the Spirit desires.
[7]The sinful mind is hostile to God. It does not submit to God's law, nor can it do so. [8]Those controlled by the sinful nature cannot please God.
[9]You, however, are controlled not by the sinful nature but by the Spirit, if the Spirit of God lives in you. And if anyone does not have the Spirit of Christ, he does not belong to Christ. [10]But if Christ is in you, your body is dead because of sin, yet your spirit is alive because of righteousness.

ROMANS 8:16 • The Spirit himself testifies with our spirit that we are God's children.

JOHN 3:19-21 • [19]"This is the verdict: Light has come into the world, but men loved darkness instead of light because their deeds were evil. [20]Everyone who does evil hates the light, and will not come into the light for fear that his deeds will be exposed. [21]But whoever lives by the truth comes into the light, so that it may be seen plainly that what he has done has been done through God."

JOHN 13:35 • "By this all men will know that you are my disciples, if you love one another."

CREATED PERFECT FOR A LOVE RELATIONSHIP •
God wanted a people with whom He could fellowship, so He created man in His own image, in His own likeness. His creation was "very good" (see Gen. 1:26-27,31). God loved His human creations and provided everything they needed in the garden of Eden. Before sin entered the world, the relationship of man and woman with God was beautiful and pure. God would come in the cool of the evening or the early morning and seek fellowship with Adam and Eve. Nothing separated them: no shame, no guilt, no fear, no despair, no depression. They had a pure fellowship and love for each other.

◆ As you read the Scriptures at the right, complete the following:

   In Genesis 1:26-27,31 underline the way God evaluated His creation.
   In Mark 12:28-30 circle the one word that best describes what God wants from His human creation. Write that word in the blank below.

God's greatest desire for us is that we _____ Him with all our being.

According to John 17:3, what did Jesus say is the goal of eternal life? _____

God's creation was very good. God's desire was that men and women would choose to walk with Him and grow in a love relationship that would last for eternity. His primary request from us is that we love Him with our total being. This relationship is eternal. According to Jesus our goal in life is to come to know God and His Son Jesus. This knowl-

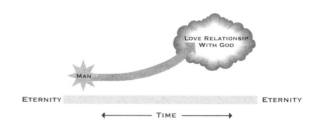

GENESIS 1:26-27,31 • 26God said, "Let us make man in our image, in our likeness. 27So God created man in his own image, in the image of God he created him; male and female he created them.
   31God saw all that he had made, and it was very good.

MARK 12:28-30 • 28One of the teachers of the law . . . asked [Jesus], "Of all the commandments, which is the most important?"
   29"The most important one," answered Jesus, "is this: 'Hear, O Israel, the Lord our God, the Lord is one. 30Love the Lord your God with all your heart and with all your soul and with all your mind and with all your strength.'"

JOHN 17:3 • Now this is eternal life: that they may know you, the only true God, and Jesus Christ, whom you have sent.

JOHN 17:3 (AMPLIFIED VERSION) • And this is eternal life: [it means] to know (to perceive, recognize, become acquainted with and understand) You, the only true and real God, and [likewise] to know Him, Jesus [as the] Christ, the Anointed One, the Messiah, Whom You have sent.

edge comes from experiencing God in a love relationship. The picture at the top of the previous page shows God's original purpose for humanity. God is at work in history from eternity past to eternity future. His primary goal for a person in this life (time) is that he or she come to know God in a personal way. This pure and intimate love relationship in time prepares us for an eternity in His presence. Time is our opportunity to get to know Him.

A BROKEN RELATIONSHIP • From the very beginning, God gave His creation the choice of life and death. Sin, disobedience, and rebellion against God's commands carried severe penalties. Adam and Eve had a choice: (1) Life in perfect fellowship with a loving Creator or (2) death for disobedience. Sadly, they chose to disobey God and suffer the consequences of their sin. Their beautiful relationship with God was broken.

◆ Read the following Scriptures and write a title for each one that summarizes the verses.

- Genesis 2:9,16-17_____ _____
- Genesis 3:6_____
- Genesis 3:8-10 _____
- Genesis 3:22-23 _____ _____

GENESIS 2:9,16-17 • 9In the middle of the garden were the tree of life and the tree of the knowledge of good and evil.

16And the Lord God commanded the man, "You are free to eat from any tree in the garden; 17but you must not eat from the tree of the knowledge of good and evil, for when you eat of it you will surely die."

GENESIS 3:6 • When the woman saw that the fruit of the tree [of knowledge of good and evil] was good for food and pleasing to the eye, and also desirable for gaining wisdom, she took some and ate it. She also gave some to her husband, who was with her, and he ate it.

GENESIS 3:8-10 • 8The man and his wife heard the sound of the Lord God as he was walking in the garden in the cool of the day, and they hid from the Lord God. 9But the Lord God called to the man, "Where are you?"
10He answered, "I heard you in the garden, and I was afraid . . . so I hid."

GENESIS 3:22-23 • 22The Lord God said, "The man . . . must not be allowed to reach out his hand and take also from the tree of life and eat, and live forever." 23So the Lord God banished him from the Garden of Eden.

ENCOUNTERING GOD IN PRAYER

Spend some time working on your relationship with God today. Adam and Eve walked with God in the garden in the cool of the day. Spend some time walking and talking with the Lord. Don't plan anything but enjoying His company. God takes pleasure in fellowshipping with you.

Day 2: God Provides Redemption

Adam and Eve chose to walk independently of God and His commands. The consequence of their sin was death. Ever since then people have chosen to sin. At some point we have all chosen to rebel against God's rule. The picture below illustrates what happens when we sin.

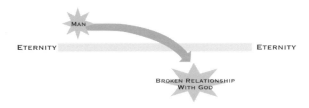

◆ Read the Scriptures in the box at the top right. Then, in the picture above, write a one- or two-word description of the result of sin (see Eph. 2:1).

Yesterday's picture showed God's desire for a love relationship with you for eternity. The picture above shows that sin causes a broken relationship with God. According to the Scriptures, because of sin, we are *dead*. We are separated from God and without hope. That is just what we deserve. Our choices to sin bring us into slavery to sin. The Bible speaks of our need to be redeemed or ransomed from this spiritual death. A price must be paid to satisfy the wages of sin. The good news of the gospel is that God has provided a way to life. He has provided for our redemption through Jesus Christ.

Romans 3:23 All have sinned and fall short of the glory of God.

Romans 6:23 The wages of sin is death.

Ephesians 2:1 As for you, you were dead in your transgressions and sins.

ROMANS 3:22-25 • [22]Righteousness from God comes through faith in Jesus Christ to all who believe. There is no difference, [23]for all have sinned and fall short of the glory of God, [24]and are justified freely by his grace through the redemption that came by Christ Jesus. [25]God presented him as a sacrifice of atonement, through faith in his blood.

EPHESIANS 1:4-8 • [4]For he chose us in him before the creation of the world to be holy and blameless in his sight. In love [5]he predestined us to be adopted as his sons through Jesus Christ, in accordance with his pleasure and will— [6]to the praise of his glorious grace, which he has freely given us in the One he loves. [7]In him we have redemption through his blood, the forgiveness of sins, in accordance with the riches of God's grace [8]that he lavished on us with all wisdom and understanding.

GOD'S SALVATION

Redemption—God's deliverance of a person from the guilt and power of sin through the death of Jesus Christ and God's placement of His life within the individual.

◆ Circle the word *redemption* in Romans 3:22-25; Ephesians 1:4-8; Colossians 1:13-14; Hebrews 9:11-12,14-15. Who provided redemption and through whom?

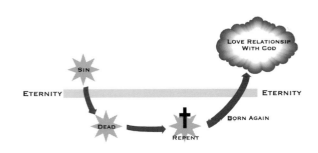

God loves His creation. It is not His desire that any perish. He wants all people to come to repentance (see 2 Pet. 3:9). So God sent His own Son Jesus to pay the death penalty for our sin. Jesus did this so that we might be saved, so that we might have life.

◆ Read the following paragraph. Label the picture that follows using the numbered statements. Write each number (1-5) on the picture.

When God saves us, He brings us back to a perfect love relationship. The picture on this page shows this process. (1) You choose to sin. (2) You are dead in sin. (3) Christ paid the ransom for your sin by His death on the cross. (4) When you repent of your sin you place your faith in Him, (5) God forgives you and restores you to a right love relationship with Him.

COLOSSIANS 1:13-14 • [13]For he has rescued us from the dominion of darkness and brought us into the kingdom of the Son he loves, [14]in whom we have redemption, the forgiveness of sins.

HEBREWS 9:11-12,14-15 • [11]When Christ came as high priest. . . . [12]He entered the Most Holy Place once for all by his own blood, having obtained eternal redemption.

[14]How much more, then, will the blood of Christ . . . cleanse our consciences from acts that lead to death, so that we may serve the living God!

[15]Christ is the mediator of a new covenant, that those who are called may receive the promised eternal inheritance—now that he has died as a ransom to set them free from the sins committed under the first covenant.

ENCOUNTERING GOD IN PRAYER

If you have not experienced God's redemption, turn to page 97 and consider repenting of your sin, trusting Jesus Christ as your Savior, and making Him Lord of your life. God wants more than anything else to have a love relationship with you. If you have experienced God's redemption, you have life in relationship with God. Worship Him. Express your love for Him. Thank Him for the sacrifice of His Son so that you may have life.

Day 3: God Chooses a People

God's plan for redemption did not begin with the coming of Jesus. Many see a promise of Jesus' victory over Satan in Genesis 3:15. About the woman's offspring, God said to the serpent, "He will crush your head." The seriousness of sin is clear. God described severe consequences for the serpent, woman, and man because of their sin.

In Genesis 12, God began to reveal His purposes in redeeming a world. He called Abram (later changed to Abraham) to become involved in His eternal purposes.

◆ Read Genesis 12:1-3.

Who is the real focus of this passage?
❏ The focus is on Abram and what he will do for God.
❏ The focus is on God and what He will do through Abram.

The primary purpose of God's call to Abram was to bless what group?
❏ God called Abram to bless him and his family.
❏ God called Abram to bless the nation of his descendants.
❏ God called Abram to bless all the peoples of the earth.

What are some things God expected of Abraham (see Gen. 17:1,7;18:18-19)?_____

_____

The focus is on God and His activity. In the call of Abram, God was setting in motion His plan to redeem the world. The reason God came to Abram was because He wanted to do it through him. God asked Abram to follow Him, to be blameless, and to teach his children to obey God. God kept His promises and made Abram's descendants a nation.

GOD CALLS ABRAHAM

GENESIS 12:1-3 • [1]The Lord had said to Abram, "Leave your country, your people and your father's household and go to the land I will show you. [2]I will make you into a great nation and I will bless you; I will make your name great, and you will be a blessing. [3]I will bless those who bless you, and whoever curses you I will curse; and all the peoples of the earth will be blessed through you."

GENESIS 17:1,7 • [1]The Lord . . . said, "I am God Almighty; walk before me and be blameless. [7]I will establish my covenant. . . between me and you and your descendants after you for the generations to come, to be your God and the God of your descendants after you."

GENESIS 18:18-19 • [18]"Abraham will surely become a great and powerful nation, and all nations on earth will be blessed through him. [19]For I have chosen him, so that he will direct his children and his household after him to keep the way of the Lord by doing what is right and just."

◆ Read about God's call of Israel in Exodus 19:3-6 and Deuteronomy 7:6-9. Pay attention to statements about the love relationship God desires with His people.

In Exodus 19:4 God powerfully delivered Israel from Egypt. Where did He lead them?

_____

In Exodus 19:5 what were God's two requirements of Israel?_____

_____

What would the nation be to God? Fill in the blanks (vv. 5-6)
My _____ possession, _____ of priests, _____ nation.
7. In Deuteronomy 7:8 what two reasons did God give for choosing Israel?_____

We usually think that God brought Israel into the promised land. God said, "I brought you to _myself._" That is what made them special. God brought them to a relationship with Himself in which they would be His treasured possession, a kingdom of priests, a holy nation. God chose them because of His love and to keep His promise to Abraham. God asked the people to obey _Him,_ not just laws and commands. He asked them to keep the covenant relationship of love with Him so that He could continue to accomplish His mighty purposes through them.

GOD'S COVENANT WITH ISRAEL

EXODUS 19:3-6 • [3]Moses went up to God, and the Lord called to him from the mountain and said, "This is what you are to say to the house of Jacob and what you are to tell the people of Israel: [4]"You yourselves have seen what I did to Egypt, and how I carried you on eagles' wings and brought you to myself. [5]Now if you obey me fully and keep my covenant, then out of all nations you will be my treasured possession. Although the whole earth is mine, [6]you will be for me a kingdom of priests and a holy nation.'"

DEUTERONOMY 7:6-9 • [6]You are a people holy to the Lord your God. The Lord your God has chosen you out of all the peoples on the face of the earth to be his people, his treasured possession.
[7]The Lord did not set his affection on you and choose you because you were more numerous than other peoples. . . . [8]But it was because the Lord loved you and kept the oath he swore to your forefathers. . . . [9]Know therefore that the Lord your God is God; he is the faithful God, keeping his covenant of love to a thousand generations of those who love him and keep his commands.

ENCOUNTERING GOD IN PRAYER
Why did God choose you to be His child? Thank God for the privilege of being adopted into His family. Talk to God about His love, your relationship with Him, and about His requirements of you.

Day 4: God's Royal Priesthood

Israel had been called by God to be a royal priesthood. God intended to work through them to draw a world to Himself. By the time Jesus came to provide for our forgiveness, Israel had departed from God again. Many had departed from their relationship with God. The religious leaders were so disoriented that they did not even recognize God. In fact, they killed Him.

In Christ, God established a new covenant with a new Israel—the church. This new relationship was based on faith and not the keeping of the law. God chose and called out a new people who responded to His offer of salvation through faith in His Son. Your Scripture memory verse describes God's people.

◆ Read 1 Peter 2:9.

What four phrases describe God's people—the church?

a. _____

b. _____

c. _____

d. _____

Which one of the four is most meaningful to you? Why? _____

For what purpose have God's people been chosen?
To declare God's

_____

God said the church is a chosen people, a royal priesthood, a holy nation, and a people belonging to God. God chose His people out of His mercy and love. His purpose for them was that they declare His praises to people living in sin.

1 PETER 2:4-5 • ⁴As you come to him, the living Stone . . . ⁵you also, like living stones, are being built into a spiritual house to be a holy priesthood, offering spiritual sacrifices acceptable to God through Jesus Christ.

> ### God's Chosen People
> You are a chosen people, a royal priesthood, a holy nation, a people belonging to God, that you may declare the praises of him who called you out of darkness into his wonderful light.
> —1 Peter 2:9

---

1 PETER 2:10 • Once you were not a people, but now you are the people of God; once you had not received mercy, but now you have received mercy.

1 PETER 2:11-12 • ¹¹I urge you . . . to abstain from sinful desires. . . . ¹²Live such good lives among the pagans that . . . they may see your good deeds and glorify God on the day he visits us.

CHOSEN. As God's people, we are chosen to be God's special treasures. We are special because we are related to Him.

ROYAL PRIESTHOOD. God did not say that they were a kingdom with a priesthood—a select few that can relate to Him. He said, "You are . . . a royal priesthood." Every single believer is a priest unto God. *Royal* means each one has direct access to the King of kings. The role of the priest was primarily to bring a word from God to the people. The priest also represented the people before God.

HOLY NATION. Not only are we a kingdom of priests, but we are to be a holy nation. The word *holy* means "set apart for God's exclusive use." We are to be separated from the common, separated from the ways of the world. We are different from the world. We are to reflect God, His nature and ways. We are commanded to be holy as He is holy.

BELONGING TO GOD. We belong to God. We are not our own; we belong to another. What a wonderful privilege we have to belong to the family of the Almighty God.

> • Are you living in the joy, wonder, and awe of being God's chosen and treasured possession? How?
>
> • How faithfully are you and members of your church practicing their priesthood before God and others?
>
> • How much time are your members spending in direct communion with the King?
>
> • How faithfully are they declaring God's praises to the world in darkness?
>
> • What are they doing as a body to represent one another's spiritual needs to God?
>
> • How separate are your members from the world and its ways? Are they holy as God is holy?

◆ Match the description on the left with the characteristic of God's people on the right.

____ 1. Related to the King of kings	a. Holy	
____ 2. Set apart for God's use	b. Priesthood	
____ 3. The object of God's love and mercy	c. Royal	
____ 4. Representing God to humanity	d. Chosen	(Answers: 1-c; 2-a; 3-d; 4-b.)

ENCOUNTERING GOD IN PRAYER

Ask God how your church measures up against His purposes for His people. Think through the questions above. Discuss with the Lord what might need to be done to become more clearly the people He intended. Write notes for sharing and discussion with your church family.

Day 5: God's Fellow Workers

In this unit you have learned that: (1) God created humanity in a perfect state. (2) Sin entered the world. (3) Because of sin, people are dead in trespasses and sin. (4) God has a mission to redeem a lost world. (5) God has chosen to work through His chosen people to carry out His redemptive plan. (6) God has provided for redemption through the death of Jesus on the cross. (7) God has called the church to be His people.

Now, God is at work through His people to accomplish His redemptive work. His goal is to exalt Jesus and draw a lost world to faith in Christ. This is summarized in Phases 1 and 7 of God's Pattern.

On the inside back cover of this book read Phase 1 and Phase 7.

◆ Read 2 Corinthians 5:11,14-15,17—6:1 to understand the ministry God has given to the church. Answer the following questions.
Who was reconciling the world to Himself? (v. 19)

_____

Through whom is God reconciling the world to Himself? ❑ Through the church ❑ Through Christ

What ministry/message has God given to the church?

_____

In verses 5:20 and 6:1, circle words that describe our job.

What should motivate us in the ministry of reconciliation? (v. 14)_____

_____

Reconciled means "restored to a right relationship." God is the One reconciling the world to Himself through Christ. Yet, God has given the ministry and message of reconciliation to the church. In that ministry we are Christ's ambassadors and God's fellow workers. Our motivation for this work is the love of Christ—He compels us by His love.

2 CORINTHIANS 5:11,14-15,17—6:1 • [11]Since, then, we know what it is to fear the Lord, we try to persuade men. . . . [14]For Christ's love compels us, because we are convinced that one died for all, and therefore all died. [15]And he died for all, that those who live should no longer live for themselves but for him who died for them and was raised again. [17]Therefore, if anyone is in Christ, he is a new creation; the old has gone, the new has come! [18]All this is from God, who reconciled us to himself through Christ and gave us the ministry of reconciliation: [19]that God was reconciling the world to himself in Christ. . . . And he has committed to us the message of reconciliation. [20]We are therefore Christ's ambassadors, as though God were making his appeal through us. We implore you on Christ's behalf: Be reconciled to God. [21]God made him who had no sin to be sin for us, so that in him we might become the righteousness of God.
[1]As God's fellow workers we urge you not to receive God's grace in vain.

◆ Read John 15:5,8, 15:16, and 14:10,12-14 to see how we relate to God in His work. How much can we accomplish for the Kingdom apart from God?

_____

In John 15:8,16 what kind of fruit does God want to bear through us? _____

Which of the following is correct? Check one.
❏ Our church chose to be part of God's work.
❏ God chose us to join Him in His work.

What kind of things will believers in Christ be able to do? (v. 12) _____

If Jesus is our example, who will be accomplishing the work? (v. 10)
❏ We will be doing the work for God, the Father.
❏ The Father will be doing His work through us.

God is the One who is on a redemptive mission. The mission is His. In God's love He has chosen the church to work together with Him in His mission. The mission is not one we can accomplish—we can do nothing apart from God. God does the work through us. When God works through us, however, we will bear much fruit for the Kingdom—fruit that will last. With God at work through His church, the church will accomplish great things.

JOHN 15:5,8 • ⁵I am the vine; you are the branches. If a man remains in me and I in him, he will bear much fruit; apart from me you can do nothing.
⁸This is to my Father's glory, that you bear much fruit, showing yourselves to be my disciples.

JOHN 15:16 • You did not choose me, but I chose you and appointed you to go and bear fruit—fruit that will last.

JOHN 14:10,12-14 • ¹⁰Don't you believe that I am in the Father, and that the Father is in me? The words I say to you are not just my own. Rather, it is the Father, living in me, who is doing his work.
¹²Anyone who has faith in me will do what I have been doing. He will do even greater things than these, because I am going to the Father. ¹³And I will do whatever you ask in my name, so that the Son may bring glory to the Father. ¹⁴You may ask me for anything in my name, and I will do it.

ENCOUNTERING GOD IN PRAYER
Ask God to guide you in evaluating the fruit of your life and that of your church. Does the fruit bring glory to your heavenly Father? Do others know you are His disciples by the fruit you bear? How much fruit are you bearing for the Kingdom? How lasting is the fruit you are bearing? What does this indicate about how well you are abiding in Him? Talk to the Lord about your love relationship and any improvement He may desire.

Unit 2 Review: God Is on Mission in Our World

◆ As a review of this unit, answer the following questions. If you need help, scan back through the unit for answers.

1. Fill in the blanks in Phase 1 below. Check your answers by referring to the inside back cover.
Phase 1: God is on _____ to _____ a lost world. God calls His _____ into a relationship with Himself, and He accomplishes His work through them.

2. Which of the following is God's *greatest* desire for us?
❑ a. God wants us to serve Him.
❑ b. God wants us to love Him.

3. What is the result of sin? Check all that apply.
❑ a. A love relationship with God   ❑ c. Life
❑ b. A broken relationship with God   ❑ d. Death

4. How did God provide for our redemption—our ransom from death?

_____

5. Who has God chosen to be His people in our day?

_____

6. What statement, Scripture, or idea has been most meaningful to you in this unit?

_____

7. Reword that statement, Scripture, or idea into a prayer response to God.

_____

_____

_____

8. Write from memory 1 Peter 2:9 describing God's chosen people.

_____

_____

_____

_____

_____

9. Based on 1 Peter 2:9, what are four ways God describes His people?

1. _____

2. _____

3. _____

4. _____

Unit 3: God's People Tend to Depart

Though God has blessed His people with every spiritual blessing, they tend to depart from Him. This begins with a subtle shift of the heart away from the love relationship with God. Once the heart shifts, God's people fail to obey Him. They begin to disobey Him. They turn to other gods—substitutes for God and the love relationship. Over a period of time God's people can move far from Him.

DAY 1: A SHIFT OF THE HEART

DAY 2: SIGNS OF A HEART SHIFT

DAY 3: CRACKED CISTERNS INSTEAD OF LIVING WATER

DAY 4: IDOLS OF THE HEART

DAY 5: SUBSTITUTES FOR GOD

LEARNING GOAL

You will understand how to know when you have departed from God and you will demonstrate your desire to deal with any area of life where you have departed from Him.

SCRIPTURE MEMORY VERSE

Hebrews 3:12-13

[12] See to it, brothers, that none of you has a sinful, unbelieving heart that turns away from the living God.
[13] But encourage one another daily.

PHASE 2:

God's people tend to depart from Him, turning to substitutes for His presence, purposes, and ways.

SUMMARY STATEMENTS

• God's Holy Spirit is in you to guide and empower you in every act of obedience.
• Moving away from God has nothing to do with activity; it has to do with a radical shift in your heart.
• Disobedience and turning to substitutes for God are clear signs that your heart has turned.
• Jesus says that it is spiritually impossible to love Him and not obey Him.
• God alone is able to fill us completely with life when He fills us with Himself.
• The Lord is your life.
• An idol is anything you substitute for God.
• Anything that captures your heart can be a substitute for God.
• A major tragedy of the Christian community is that we are filled with substitutes we have chosen for God. We have often substituted work, ritual or traditional religious activity, relationships with others, or a love for the things of the world for a love relationship with God.

First Great Awakening

GREAT NEED • The First Great Awakening in the American colonies is often dated 1740-43. Like other great revivals, the spiritual climate of the churches had reached a low point. Practices like the Half-Way Covenant brought many into church membership without requiring any indication of saving faith. Consequently, churches were a mixture of believers and unbelievers. The vitality of the Christian testimony was watered down by its mixture with the world.

FAR REACHING RESULTS • Traveling evangelists like George Whitefield and Gilbert Tennent were used by God to quicken the spirits of His people. Through their preaching many church members and even preachers came under the conviction of the Holy Spirit that they had never been converted. They were greatly distressed until they had made their salvation sure. Historians estimate that 25,000 to 50,000 persons were added to the churches in New England alone—amounting to 7-14 percent of the population. New churches were started in record numbers, and colleges like Dartmouth and Princeton began to train missionaries and ministers to carry the gospel to the lost world. This revival also laid the foundation of cooperative relationships between denominations. The religious liberties guaranteed in the new republic had their birth in this revival.

REVIVAL AT NORTHAMPTON • Sometime around 1734 revival began to occur in several locations in New England. God used these early revivals and awakenings to prepare the "soil" of New England for the sowing of the gospel that would follow.

Northampton, Massachusetts, was the site of a citywide awakening in 1734-35. Jonathan Edwards was pastor of the Congregational church. Prior to the revival the town experienced a "degenerate time" with a "dullness of religion." According to Edwards, the young people were addicted to nightwalking, tavern drinking, lewd practices, and frolics among the sexes the greater part of the night. "Family government did too much fail in the town." And for a long period the town was sharply divided between two parties who were jealous of each other in all public affairs.

In a nearby village two young people died in the spring of 1734. People began to think soberly about spiritual and eternal matters. In answer to the prayers of His people, God began to move. In the fall Edwards preached on justification by faith alone. In December of 1734, five or six persons were converted. One of them was a young woman who was "one of the greatest company keepers in the whole town." Her life was so radically changed that everyone could tell it was a work of God's grace. During the following six months, 300 people were "hopefully" converted in this town of 1,100.

Edwards said, "God has also seemed to have gone out of his usual way in the quickness of his work, and the swift progress his Spirit has made in his operation, on the hearts of many" (p. 239). "There was scarcely a single person in the town, either old or young, that was left unconcerned about the great things of the eternal world. . . . The town seemed to be full of the presence of God: it never was so full of love, nor so full of joy. . . . It was a time of joy in families on the account of salvation's being brought unto them. . . . Our public assemblies were then beautiful; the congregation was alive in God's service, every one earnestly intent on the public worship. . . . Our public praises were then greatly enlivened; God was then served . . . in the beauty of holiness." (p. 235)

Would you like to see God sweep your city or town and church like that? Would you be willing to pray: "God, whatever it takes for you to bring revival to your people, please do it!"?

This account has been adapted from "Narrative of Surprising Conversions" by Jonathan Edwards in *The Works of President Edwards*, New York: Leavitt & Allen, 1857 (pp. 231-272); and *The History of American Revivals* by Frank Grenville Beardsley, 1912 (pp. 20-83).

Cleansing by Washing with Water Through the Word

> *Christ loved the church and gave himself up for her to make her holy, cleansing her by the washing with water through the word, and to present her to himself as a radiant church, without stain or wrinkle or any other blemish, but holy and blameless.*
> —*Ephesians 5:25-27*

Read and pray through the following Scriptures this week. Let God speak to you through His Word. Use arrows to mark items to "wash out" or "wash in" to your life.

WASH OUT: Are there actions, behaviors, habits, or sins that need to be "washed out" of your life? your family? your church? Confess them (agree with God about the wrong) and turn away from them and to God.

WASH IN: Are there good things God wants to "wash into" your life? your family? your church? Pray about those and become all God wants you to be.

ROMANS 12:1-2 • [1]I urge you, brothers, in view of God's mercy, to offer your bodies as living sacrifices, holy and pleasing to God— this is your spiritual act of worship. [2]Do not conform any longer to the pattern of this world, but be transformed by the renewing of your mind. Then you will be able to test and approve what God's will is—his good, pleasing and perfect will.

MATTHEW 5:21-24 • [21]"You have heard that it was said to the people long ago, 'Do not murder, and anyone who murders will be subject to judgment.' [22]But I tell you that anyone who is angry with his brother will be subject to judgment. [23]"Therefore, if you are offering your gift at the altar and there remember that your brother has something against you, [24]leave your gift there in front of the altar. First go and be reconciled to your brother; then come and offer your gift."

MATTHEW 5:27-28 • [27]"You have heard that it was said, 'Do not commit adultery.' [28]But I tell you that anyone who looks at a woman lustfully has already committed adultery with her in his heart."

MATTHEW 5:31-32 • [31]"It has been said, 'Anyone who divorces his wife must give her a certificate of divorce.' [32]But I tell you that anyone who divorces his wife, except for marital unfaithfulness, causes her to become an adulteress, and anyone who marries the divorced woman commits adultery."

MATTHEW 5:33-34,37 • [33]"You have heard that it was said to the people long ago, 'Do not break your oath, but keep the oaths you have made to the Lord.' [34]But I tell you, Do not swear at all. . . . [37]Simply let your 'Yes' be 'Yes,' and your 'No,' 'No'; anything beyond this comes from the evil one."

PSALM 1:1-2 • [1]Blessed is the man who does not walk in the counsel of the wicked or stand in the way of sinners or sit in the seat of mockers. [2]But his delight is in the law of the Lord, and on his law he meditates day and night.

2 TIMOTHY 3:1-5 • [1]There will be terrible times in the last days. [2]People will be lovers of themselves, lovers of money, boastful, proud, abusive, disobedient to their parents, ungrateful, unholy, [3]without love, unforgiving, slanderous, without self-control, brutal, not lovers of the good, [4]treacherous, rash, conceited, lovers of pleasure rather than lovers of God—[5]having a form of godliness but denying its power.

TITUS 3:9-10 • [9]Avoid foolish controversies and genealogies and arguments and quarrels about the law, because these are unprofitable and useless. [10]Warn a divisive person once, and then warn him a second time. After that, have nothing to do with him. [11]You may be sure that such a man is warped and sinful; he is self-condemned.

Day 1: A Shift of the Heart

In Unit 2 you studied the first phase in God's Pattern. In this unit you will study Phase 2.

◆ Fill in the blanks in Phase 1 below. Check your answers by referring to inside the back cover.

Phase 1: *God is on _____ to _____ a lost world. God calls His _____ into a relationship with Himself, and He accomplishes His work through them.*

Referring to the inside back cover, fill in the key words in Phase 2.

Phase 2: *God's people tend to _____ from _____, turning to substitutes for His _____, _____, and _____.*

Turn to page 20 and read again the Scriptures from Judges 2 that describe a cycle of sin. What did the people do in stage 2 of the cycle?
The people _____

God has created us and called us into a love relationship with Himself. God has called us to be on mission with Him in redeeming a lost world. Without God that is an impossible mission. With God, however, all things are possible. We often forsake or leave our relationship with God.

◆ Read Deuteronomy 30:11-16. How difficult is knowing and obeying God's commands? (vv. 11-14)

_____

[11]Now what I am commanding you today is not too difficult for you or beyond your reach. [12]It is not up in heaven, so that you have to ask, "Who will ascend into heaven to get it and proclaim it to us so we may obey it?" [13]Nor is it beyond the sea, so that you have to ask, "Who will cross the sea to get it and proclaim it to us so we may obey it?" [14]No, the word is very near you; it is in your mouth and in your heart so you may obey it.

[15]See, I set before you today life and prosperity, death and destruction. [16]For I command you today to love the Lord your God, to walk in his ways, and to keep his commands, decrees and laws; then you will live and increase, and the Lord your God will bless you in the land you are entering to possess.

[17]But if your heart turns away and you are not obedient, and if you are drawn away to bow down to other gods and worship them, [18]I declare to you this day that you will certainly be destroyed. You will not live long in the land you are crossing the Jordan to enter and possess.

[19]This day I call heaven and earth as witnesses against you that I have set before you life and death, blessings and curses. Now choose life, so that you and your children may live [20]and that you may love the Lord your God, listen to his voice, and hold fast to him. For the Lord is your life.

Where is God's word for you? (v. 14)

_____

What three things does God command us to do in verse 16?

_____

_____

_____

In this passage God asks us to do three things: (1) love Him; (2) walk in His ways; and (3) keep His commands, decrees, and laws. More than anything else God wants you to love Him. God wants you to do things His way rather than your own way or the world's way. God wants you to obey Him. God's commands are given to provide you a meaningful life. His will is not hidden so that you need a religious specialist to explain His word to you. As a Christian, God's Holy Spirit is present _in you_ to guide you and empower you in every act of obedience.

God has "blessed us . . . with every spiritual blessing" (see Eph. 1:3). With all that God has done for us, we still tend to depart from Him. The process of moving away from God is clearly stated in the Scriptures. How does a person move away from God? How does a church move away from God?

◆ Read Deuteronomy 30:17-20. Where does turning away from God begin?

_____

What steps do we follow when we depart from the Lord? Fill in the blanks from verse 17.
_"If your _____ turns away and you are _____, and if you are _____ to bow down to other _____ and worship them."_

What two options does God give us? Circle them in verse 19.

Based on verse 20, which of the following is correct?
❑ The Lord gives us life.
❑ The Lord Himself is our life.

Moving away from God has nothing to do with activity. It has to do with a radical shift in your heart. Departing from God follows a progression. It begins with a shift of your heart away from Him. Then you disobey God. Next you turn to substitutes for Him—you worship other gods.

This passage was a warning to God's people. In love He wanted them to choose life and prosperity, not death and destruction. Notice that God gave only two options. There is no compromising position. God wants a love relationship with you. The Scripture doesn't say that the Lord will give you life. It says the Lord _is_ your life!

ENCOUNTERING GOD IN PRAYER
Read Ephesians 1:3-14. Pray as you read. Praise God for who He is. Thank God for what He has done for you. Express your love to God.

45

Day 2: Signs of a Heart Shift

STEPS OF DEPARTURE • Yesterday, we saw a progression of three steps we take in departing from God. Usually by the time God gets our attention, we have been going that way for a long time. As a marriage does not end in divorce because of one event, so we don't move away from God suddenly. It usually takes time—a period of neglect, carelessness, or rebellious choices. The symptoms may have been present in our lives or churches for a long time, but somehow we fail to pay attention until we are far away from God.

◆ According to Deuteronomy 30:17 (right), what is the order of our departure? Number the steps of departure 1-2-3 in the order they occur.
_____ We turn to substitutes for God and worship other gods.
_____ We disobey God.
_____ We allow our hearts to turn away from God.

First, we allow our hearts to turn away. Then we do not obey. Finally, we begin turning to substitutes for God. We accept substitutes for His presence, purposes, and ways. We take small steps away from God. Then suddenly we realize we have departed and are far from God. We realize we have left our love relationship with Him. We no longer love God with all our hearts.

SIGNS OF A HEART SHIFT • How do you know if your heart has shifted as an individual or as a church? *Disobedience* and *turning to substitutes for God* are two signs that are clear indicators that it has. Like a doctor looks for symptoms of the real problem, you can look for disobedience and substitutes for God as indications of a problem with your love

DEUTERONOMY 30:17 • But if your heart turns away and you are not obedient, and if you are drawn away to bow down to other gods and worship them. . . .

JOHN 14:15,21,23,24 • [15]"If you love me, you will obey what I command."
[21]"Whoever has my commands and obeys them, he is the one who loves me."
[23]"If anyone loves me, he will obey my teaching."
[24]"He who does not love me will not obey my teaching."

REVELATION 2:4-5 • [4]"I hold this against you: You have forsaken your first love. [5]Remember the height from which you have fallen! Repent and do the things you did at first. If you do not repent, I will come to you and remove your lampstand from its place."

DEUTERONOMY 30:19-20 • [19]Now choose life, so that you and your children may live [20]and that you may love the Lord your God, listen to his voice, and hold fast to him. For the Lord is your life.

HEBREWS 3:12-13 • [12]See to it, brothers, that none of you has a sinful, unbelieving heart that turns away from the living God. [13]But encourage one another daily.

(Answers to matching exercise on the next page: 1-b; 2-d; 3-a; 4-c)

for God. This unit will help you identify some of the signs of one who has departed from the Lord.

◆ What are two signs that your heart has shifted away from God?

1. _____ 2. _____

Read the Scriptures from John 14. Complete the statements below by correctly matching the numbered beginning with the lettered ending.

___ 1. A person who loves God   a. loves God

___ 2. A person who does not love God   b. obeys God

___ 3. A person who obeys God   c. does not love God

___ 4. A person who does not obey God   d. does not obey God

Jesus said that it is spiritually impossible to love God and not obey Him. The problem is not obedience, the problem is love. Love will always obey. But, we protest strongly and say, "Lord, it's not that I don't love You; it's that I'm having difficulty obeying You." And God would say, "If you are having difficulty obeying Me, it is because you do not love Me." If you do not understand that, you will always be trying to get right with God. You will try to reform your behavior, and you will fail.

◆ Read the Scriptures indicated and answer these questions in the right-hand column.

Why is returning to your first love for God important? (Rev. 2:4-5)

What three things can you do to choose life? (Deut. 30:19-20).

Who is your life?

What words are used in Hebrews 3:12 to describe a heart that turns away from God?

If you return to your first love—a love relationship with God—it will resolve the obedience problems in your life. "Live by the Spirit, and you will not gratify the desires of the sinful nature" (Gal. 5:16).

Is there something that God asks of you that you have done without any question, but now you question it? When Christ gives a command in His Word and you start to argue with Him, you give evidence that your heart has shifted.

◆ What is the evidence of your love for God?
❏ Saying we love Him
❏ Obeying Him

We have observed churches that sincerely sought the will of God. Many members clearly sensed a direction from God. Some in the church, however, raised such a storm of protest that they did not obey. The heart of the church had begun to shift. The next time the church sensed God's directions, they still didn't obey. Then the heart of the church began to harden.

ENCOUNTERING GOD IN PRAYER

If God evaluated your obedience record right now, what would He conclude about your love for Him? Ask the Holy Spirit to reveal ways you may not be obeying God. Start making a list of anything God brings to mind. Ask God to shed light on the quality of your love relationship with Him.

Day 3: Cracked Cisterns Instead of Living Water

In Deuteronomy 30 we saw a three-step process of departing from God. (1) The heart shifts, (2) we disobey, and (3) we turn to substitutes for God.

◆ Read about Israel's departure in Jeremiah 2:2-13. As you read, try to hear the broken heart of God as He describes the way His people left Him. Underline and number the two sins God charged His people with committing (v. 13).

God has created us with a big emptiness that only He can fill. God is the living Water. God is like a well that springs up out of the ground. God alone is able to fill us completely with life when He fills us with Himself. Life is a Person—"The Lord is your life" (Deut. 30:20). Jesus said, "I am. . . the life" (John 14:6). Even today we commit two sins: we forsake God—the living Water—and try to come up with substitutes (broken cisterns/containers) for Him. The tragedy is that our substitutes are cracked. They cannot provide life, and they cannot hold life from other sources.

THE WOMAN AT THE WELL • On a trip through Samaria, Jesus stopped to rest at Jacob's well near the town of Sychar. A woman came to draw water, and Jesus asked her for a drink. Jesus knew that the woman had looked for fullness of life in substitutes for God. He led her into a discussion of living water.

◆ Read part of the story of the Samaritan woman at the well in John 4. What had the woman turned to as substitutes for a relationship with God?

JEREMIAH 2:2-13 • [God speaking to Israel] ²"I remember the devotion of your youth, how as a bride you loved me and followed me. . . . ³Israel was holy to the Lord."

⁵"What fault did your fathers find in me, that they strayed so far from me? ⁶They did not ask, 'Where is the Lord?'

⁷"I brought you into a fertile land to eat its fruit and rich produce. But you came and defiled my land and made my inheritance detestable. ⁸The priests did not ask, 'Where is the Lord?' Those who deal with the law did not know me; the leaders rebelled against me. The prophets prophesied by Baal, following worthless idols.

⁹"Therefore I bring charges against you again," declares the Lord. . . . ¹⁰"Cross over to the coasts . . . and observe closely; see if there has ever been anything like this: ¹¹Has a nation ever changed its gods? (Yet they are not gods at all.) But my people have exchanged their Glory for worthless idols. ¹²Be appalled at this, O heavens, and shudder with great horror," declares the Lord.

¹³"My people have committed two sins: They have forsaken me, the spring of living water, and have dug their own cisterns, broken cisterns that cannot hold water."

PEOPLE • The Samaritan woman tried to find a husband who could fill the void in her life. That is a job too big for any human. When one husband couldn't meet her deepest needs, she looked for another. By the time she met Jesus she was living with a sixth man in a sexual relationship outside of marriage.

People can become substitutes for God. Sexual relationships can become a substitute for a love relationship with God. Neither can satisfy the spiritual thirst for the Living Water—God Himself.

RITUAL WORSHIP • The Samaritan woman also discussed religious worship with Jesus. Did you notice that the focus of her question was not on God? She was concerned about the *place* of worship. She was concerned about external things. Evidently, worship for her was just a set of traditional religious activities. Worship was not a vital relationship with God.

Religious activity and tradition can become a substitute for a relationship with God. We can exchange a vital relationship with a living Lord for a set of religious activities. We can be busy going through the motions of religion and never experience life in Him.

JOHN 4: THE WOMAN AT THE WELL

[10]Jesus answered her, "If you knew the gift of God and who it is that asks you for a drink, you would have asked him and he would have given you living water.

[13]"Everyone who drinks this water will be thirsty again, [14]but whoever drinks the water I give him will never thirst. Indeed, the water I give him will become in him a spring of water welling up to eternal life."

[15]The woman said to him, "Sir, give me this water so that I won't get thirsty and have to keep coming here to draw water."

[16]He told her, "Go, call your husband and come back."

[17]"I have no husband," she replied.

Jesus said to her, "You are right when you say you have no husband. [18]The fact is, you have had five husbands, and the man you now have is not your husband.

[19]"Sir," the woman said, "I can see that you are a prophet. [20]Our fathers worshiped on this mountain, but you Jews claim that the place where we must worship is in Jerusalem."

[21]Jesus declared, "Believe me, woman, a time is coming when you will worship the Father neither on this mountain nor in Jerusalem. . . . [23]a time is coming and has now come when the true worshippers will worship the Father in spirit and truth.

ENCOUNTERING GOD IN PRAYER

Is your love relationship with God real, personal, practical, and intimate? Or is there an emptiness, a dryness, dullness, apathy, indifference, or boredom about your relationship with Him? Have you turned to substitutes that have robbed you of the vital relationship to God? Ask God to begin helping you identify anything (and everything) in your life that has become a substitute for Him. If God begins to identify things, write them down—Knowing what they are will prepare you to deal with them later in our study.

Day 4: Idols of the Heart

The Scriptures are filled with examples of people who chose substitutes for God. Throughout history God's people have tended to turn to substitutes for their relationship with God. Don't think that you are not vulnerable as well. Anytime you turn to anyone or anything when you should turn to God, you make that person or thing an idol. An idol is anything you substitute for God. It does not have to be an image set up in your home to worship. The Scriptures also describe idols of the heart.

◆ Read Ezekiel 14:3-6. Circle the words idol(s) and heart(s) each time they occur.
Where did the people set up these idols?

_____

What had Israel done to God (v. 5)?

_____

What was God planning to do to Israel (v. 5)?

_____

The people had set up idols "in their hearts and . . . before their faces." By setting up idols, they had deserted God. Their hearts had shifted. So God was planning to recapture the hearts of His people. Isn't it sad to think that, after all God had done for Israel, He had to work to win back their love? Could that be true of us? After all God has done for us in Christ, is it possible that we, too, have set up idols in our hearts?

COMMON IDOLS • In yesterday's lesson, the story of the woman at the well pointed to some substitutes for God. People, sexual relationships, and even religious activity can be idols. Let's look at some common "idols" or substitutes for God.

◆ Read Ephesians 5:3,5 and circle the names of three sins that are considered idolatry in God's sight.

According to God's Word, sexual immorality, impurity, and greed are idols of the heart. Each of these could be a one-time act, or they could be a regular practice or attitude of life. The regular practice or attitude is the sin that is idolatry. In each of these sins a person gives his heart to something other than God. A person who practices these sins has departed from God.

EZEKIEL 14:3-6 • ³These [elders of Israel] have set up idols in their hearts and put wicked stumbling blocks before their faces. . . . ⁴"When any Israelite sets up idols in his heart . . . and then goes to a prophet, I the Lord will answer him myself in keeping with his great idolatry. ⁵I will do this to recapture the hearts of the people of Israel, who have all deserted me for their idols."
⁶Therefore say to the house of Israel, "This is what the Sovereign Lord says: Repent! Turn from your idols and renounce all your detestable practices!"

EPHESIANS 5:3,5 • ³Among you there must not be even a hint of sexual immorality, or of any kind of impurity, or of greed, because these are improper for God's holy people.
⁵For of this you can be sure: No immoral, impure or greedy person—such a man is an idolater—has any inheritance in the kingdom of Christ and of God.

◆ Below are some other things that can become substitutes for a love relationship with God. Read through the list. Then read the Scriptures below. On the line beside each Scripture, write the letter of the substitute(s) that it describes. Some Scriptures may describe more than one.

a. Materialism, things of the world
b. Bible study
c. Relationships with other people
d. Career, job, work
e. Love and devotion to money
f. Ritual worship
g. Trusting in the help of others
h. Self

___JEREMIAH 17:5 • ⁵This is what the Lord says: "Cursed is the one who trusts in man, who depends on flesh for his strength and whose heart turns away from the Lord.

___MATTHEW 15:8-9 • ⁸"These people honor me with their lips, but their hearts are far from me. ⁹They worship me in vain; their teachings are but rules taught by men."

___MATTHEW 6:24 • "No one can serve two masters. Either he will hate the one and love the other, or he will be devoted to the one and despise the other. You cannot serve both God and Money."

___MATTHEW 10:37 • "Anyone who loves his father or mother more than me is not worthy of me; anyone who loves his son or daughter more than me is not worthy of me."

___LUKE 9:23-24 • ²³"If anyone would come after me, he must deny himself and take up his cross daily and follow me. ²⁴For whoever wants to save his life will lose it, but whoever loses his life for me will save it."

___JOHN 5:39-40 • ³⁹"You diligently study the Scriptures because you think that by them you possess eternal life. These are the Scriptures that testify about me, ⁴⁰yet you refuse to come to me to have life."

___ 1 JOHN 2:15-16 • ¹⁵Do not love the world or anything in the world. If anyone loves the world, the love of the Father is not in him. ¹⁶Everything in the world—the cravings of sinful man, the lust of his eyes and the boasting of what he has and does—comes not from the Father but from the world.

Do some of these surprise you? People, things, or activities may be very good. However, if we allow anything to take the place of our love of God, our heart has shifted. This is certainly not a complete list of things we can substitute for a love relationship with God. Anything that captures our heart—our love—can be a substitute for God.

Day 5: Substitutes for God

A major tragedy of the Christian community is that we continually choose substitutes for God. We have often substituted work, ritual or traditional religious activity, relationships with others, or a love for the things of the world for a love relationship with God.

PROSPERITY • A Christian leader in China told a visiting pastor from the United States, "Christians in China are praying for our Christian brothers and sisters in America. We believe we are handling our persecution better than you are handling your prosperity." Have we allowed our prosperity and materialism to become a substitute for God?

◆ Read Deuteronomy 8:10-14. What is the danger of prosperity? (v. 11)

_____

What happens to the heart that causes you to forget God? (v. 14) _____
Read Deuteronomy 8:19. What is the penalty for turning to other gods and worshiping them?

_____

The danger of prosperity or success, like any other substitute, is that it can cause us to forget God. That may be a good way to determine things that have become substitutes for God. Ask yourself if anything is causing you to forget God. In the case of prosperity or success, pride creeps into the heart. Then self claims credit for the wealth or success. Jesus said, "Watch out! Be on your guard against all kinds of greed; a man's life does not consist in the abundance of his possessions" (Luke 12:15).

God's promise of destruction for going after other gods reveals how seriously God treats sin and rebellion. The Scripture says God is jealous of our love. God created us, and He deserves our love and life. Next week we will look at the love of God that is revealed in the discipline of His people.

NOTE • *You may notice that we frequently will be studying passages from Deuteronomy. Don't discount these as "Old Testament" and therefore no longer valid for the Christian. Jesus quoted extensively from Deuteronomy as He taught the first disciples. Jesus saw great value in studying and memorizing Deuteronomy. This book tells us much about God and how He relates to His people. We can gain great value from meeting God in its pages.*

DEUTERONOMY 8:10-14 • ¹⁰**When you have eaten and are satisfied, praise the Lord your God for the good land he has given you. ¹¹Be careful that you do not forget the Lord your God, failing to observe his commands. ¹²Otherwise, when you eat and are satisfied, when you build fine houses and settle down, ¹³and when your herds and flocks grow large and your silver and gold increase and all you have is multiplied, ¹⁴then your heart will become proud and you will forget the Lord your God.**

DEUTERONOMY 8:19 • If you ever forget the Lord your God and follow other gods and worship and bow down to them, I testify against you today that you will surely be destroyed.

Every time a believer moves away from God, he puts a substitute in God's place. We replace that which we no longer have from God with something from the world. What a great tragedy this is.

◆ Read the Scriptures below. Underline things we can do that become substitutes for God.

PSALM 20:7 • Some trust in chariots and some in horses, but we trust in the name of the Lord our God.

PROVERBS 3:5-6 • ⁵Trust in the Lord with all your heart and lean not on your own understanding; ⁶in all your ways acknowledge him, and he will make your paths straight.

ISAIAH 30:1 • "Woe to the obstinate children," declares the Lord, "to those who carry out plans that are not mine, forming an alliance, but not by my Spirit."

◆ As you read the following examples, place a check beside the ones you sense may be true of you, your family, or your church.

SUBSTITUTES FOR GOD'S PRESENCE
❏ We recognize the importance of methods, programs, and people as they are used by God to accomplish spiritual and church growth, and yet we may place our complete trust in them rather than trusting God.

❏ There is a place for emotion, pageantry, and ritual, and yet we may substitute emotional hype, pageantry, entertainment, or ritual for the reality of God's intimate presence in worship.

SUBSTITUTES FOR GOD'S PURPOSES
❏ We may conduct baptism and the Lord's Supper as tradition or ritual when God intended them to be times of public testimony, remembrance of Him, personal examination, and renewal of fellowship with Him.
❏ We may spend much of our time and resources on selfish pleasures and ignore God's concerns for justice for the oppressed or meeting the needs of the poor.
❏ We may conduct "evangelistic" visits primarily to ask people to come to church for an attendance goal when God wants them to come to Him for redemption.

SUBSTITUTES FOR GOD'S WAYS
❏ We walk by sight when God says, "Walk by faith."
❏ We affirm self and give self first consideration when God says deny self.
❏ We exalt self when God says humble yourself.
❏ We try to save our lives—hold on to what we have, when God tells us to lose our lives—to give away what we have for the Kingdom's sake.
❏ We try to manipulate people to serve when God says pray that He will call forth laborers.

ENCOUNTERING GOD IN PRAYER
As you read this list, did you sense any guilt for turning to substitutes rather than God? Isn't it easy to fall into those traps? If you sensed guilt, that was the Holy Spirit. That is His job. Confess your sinful heart to the Lord and turn from any wicked way.

Unit 3 Review: God Is on Mission in Our World

As a review of this unit, answer the following questions. If you need help, scan back through the unit for answers.

1. Fill in the blanks in Phase 2 below. Check your answers by referring to the inside back cover.
Phase 2: God's people tend to _____ from _____ turning to substitutes for His _____, _____, and _____.

2. According to Deuteronomy 30:17, what are three steps we take in departing from God? (p. 45)
(1)_____(2)_____(3)_____

3. What are two signs that your heart has departed from the Lord? _____
_____

4. Give one example of a substitute for each of the following: (p. 53)
a. a substitute for God's presence:_____
b. a substitute for God's purposes:_____
c. a substitute for God's ways:_____

5. What statement, Scripture, or idea has been most meaningful to you in this unit?
_____

6. Reword that statement, Scripture, or idea into a prayer response to God. _____

7. Write from memory Hebrews 3:12-13 describing a heart that departs. _____
_____
_____
_____
_____

8. Based on Hebrews 3:12, what kind of heart should we avoid? _____

9. What can we do to help each other avoid a sinful, unbelieving heart? _____
_____

Unit 4: God Disciplines His People in Love

When God's people depart from Him, God is grieved. God knows that His people miss out on the fullness of life He intends for them when they depart from Him. God disciplines His people out of love with a desire to draw them back into a right relationship with Himself. During this unit you will study examples of the ways God disciplines and judges His people.

> **DAY 1: GOD'S NATURE**
> **DAY 2: GOD'S PURPOSE IN DISCIPLINE**
> **DAY 3: NATURE OF GOD'S DISCIPLINE AND JUDGMENT**
> **DAY 4: EXAMPLES OF GOD'S DISCIPLINES AND JUDGMENTS**
> **DAY 5: REVIVAL UNDER ASA AND AZARIAH**

LEARNING GOAL

You will understand the nature of God's discipline of His people and demonstrate an openness to God's corrective discipline in your life, family, and church.

SCRIPTURE MEMORY VERSE

Hebrews 12:5-6
[5]"Do not make light of the Lord's discipline, and do not lose heart when he rebukes you, [6]because the Lord disciplines those he loves, and he punishes everyone he accepts as a son."

PHASE 3:
God disciplines His people out of His love for them.

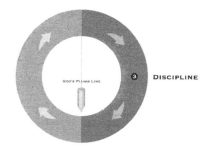

SUMMARY STATEMENTS

- God is perfect love. God forever convinced us of His love through the death of Jesus on the cross.
- God is just. His judgments are always right and fair.
- God is holy and pure. He cannot tolerate sin.
- We need to develop a healthy fear of our Holy God.
- God knows we are missing out on the life for which He created us. Because of His love, God disciplines His people when we depart from Him and sin against Him.
- Final judgments usually come after prolonged periods of sin without repentance.
- God's desire is to correct us so that we will return to Him.
- When we don't judge ourselves and repent, He judges us. God's disciplines will increase until He gets our attention.
- God is merciful and patient.

Second Great Awakening

A CALL TO PRAYER • The Second Great Awakening began in England around 1792. It had its roots in The Call to Prayer of 1784. The pastors of the Northhamptonshire Association issued a call to prayer for the first Monday of each month. Prayer meetings began to spread to other areas and across denominational lines. The object of the prayer concerts was:

That the Holy Spirit may be poured down on our ministers and churches, that sinners may be converted, the saints edified, the interest of religion revived, and the name of God glorified. At the same time . . . let the whole interest of the Redeemer be affectionately remembered, and the spread of the Gospel to the most distant parts of the habitable globe be the object of your most fervent requests.

Revival did come to ministers and churches. Word of the revival spread across the Atlantic, and by 1797 the revival fires began to break out in the United States. This awakening was different from the first. Rather than outside evangelists, God worked through pastors in their congregations.

PASTOR-LED, WORD-CENTERED, AND LONG-LIVED • Pastors preached from God's Word with a focus on God's sovereignty and the necessity of redemption. The Holy Spirit brought deep conviction of sin, and people surrendered to Christ and were converted. These revivals were long lasting covering two to three decades. Revivals swept many college campuses like Yale where 75 out of 230 students were converted. Half of those surrendered to the gospel ministry.

CAMP MEETINGS • By 1800 the movement crossed the mountains to Kentucky and Tennessee. James McGready preached in open-air meetings (later known as camp meetings). The presence of a holy God so gripped people that they experienced physical anguish often resulting in collapse, groans, and piercing shrieks. Individuals confessed their sins, prayed fervently for forgiveness and salvation, and were joyously converted.

RESULTS OF REVIVAL AND AWAKENING • This period of spiritual quickening lasted for decades and thoroughly covered Britain and the United States spreading to other countries around the globe. Lives and communities were so transformed in morals and spirit that outside observers were struck by the radical differences they saw. College campuses were reclaimed from religious infidelity to once again prepare missionaries and ministers of the gospel. Churches were revived in spirit and flooded with new converts. No one has been able to estimate the total results of the awakening, but in Kentucky, Baptists saw an increase of 10,000. The Methodist Episcopal church saw a national increase of 40,000 between 1800 and 1803. Many other denominations experienced similar growth.

MODERN MISSIONS • Perhaps the greatest impact of God's sovereign work was the launching of the modern missions movement. William Carey began his preaching ministry in the Northhamptonshire Association during the days of the Call to Prayer. In 1792 he led the organization of the Baptist Missionary Society and went to India as its first missionary. Other organizations coming to life during this time included: London Missionary Society; Congregational, Baptist, and Methodist foreign missions societies; home missions societies of several denominations; national and international Bible and tract societies; numerous Christian colleges; 17 theological seminaries; and many more.

When God's people are revived, He gives them a new heart with His compassion for a lost world.

This account has been adapted from *The History of American Revivals* by Frank Grenville Beardsley, 1912 (pp. 84-107) and "The Prayer Call of 1784" by E. A. Payne in *Ter-Jubilee Celebrations 1942-44*, Baptist Missionary Society, 1945 (pp. 19-31).

Cleansing by Washing with Water Through the Word

> *Christ loved the church and gave himself up for her to make her holy, cleansing her by the washing with water through the word, and to present her to himself as a radiant church, without stain or wrinkle or any other blemish, but holy and blameless.*
>
> —Ephesians 5:25-27

Read and pray through the following Scriptures this week. Let God speak to you through His Word.

WASH OUT: Are there actions, behaviors, habits, or sins that need to be "washed out" of your life? your family? your church? Confess them (agree with God about the wrong) and turn away from them and to God.

WASH IN: Are there good things God wants to "wash into" your life? your family? your church? Pray about those and become all God wants you to be.

HEBREWS 10:26-31 • [26]**If we deliberately keep on sinning after we have received the knowledge** of the truth, no sacrifice for sins is left, [27]**but only a fearful expectation** of judgment and of raging fire that will **consume the enemies** of God. [28]Anyone who rejected the law of Moses **died without** mercy on the testimony of two or three witnesses. [29]**How much more** severely do you think a man **deserves to be punished who** has trampled the Son of God under foot, **who has treated as an** unholy thing the blood of the covenant that **sanctified him, and** who has insulted the Spirit of grace? [30]**For we know him who said**, "It is mine to avenge; I will repay," and again, "**The Lord will** judge his people." [31]It is a dreadful thing to fall into the hands of the living God.

HEBREWS 13:4 • [4]**Marriage should** be honored by all, and the marriage bed kept pure, for God will judge the adulterer and all the sexually immoral.

2 PETER 3:3,7,11-12,14-15 • [3]In the last days scoffers will come, scoffing and following their own evil desires. [7]The present heavens and earth are reserved for fire, being kept for the day of judgment and destruction of ungodly men. [11]Since everything will be destroyed in this way, what kind of people ought you to be? You ought to live holy and godly lives [12]as you look forward to the day of God and speed its coming. [14]Since you are looking forward to this, make every effort to be found spotless, blameless and at peace with him. [15]Bear in mind that our Lord's patience means salvation.

ROMANS 6:2,6-7,11-13,16,22. • [2]We died to sin; how can we live in it any longer? [6]For we know that our old self was crucified with him so that the body of sin might be done away with, that we should no longer be slaves to sin— [7]because anyone who has died has been freed from sin. [11]Count yourselves dead to sin but alive to God in Christ Jesus. [12]Therefore do not let sin reign in your mortal body so that you obey its evil desires. [13]Do not offer the parts of your body to sin, as instruments of wickedness, but rather offer yourselves to God, as those who have been brought from death to life; and offer the parts of your body to him as instruments of righteousness. [16]Don't you know that when you offer yourselves to someone to obey him as slaves, you are slaves to the one whom you obey—whether you are slaves to sin, which leads to death, or to obedience, which leads to righteousness? [22]But now that you have been set free from sin and have become slaves to God, the benefit you reap leads to holiness, and the result is eternal life.

JAMES 5:9 • Don't grumble against each other, brothers, or you will be judged. The Judge is standing at the door!

Day 1: God's Nature

Many of God's people have lost the sense of the fear of God. We no longer believe that God holds us accountable. We don't believe God disciplines and judges His people. Many think that the God of judgment and wrath was the God we see in the Old Testament. They think of God revealed in the New Testament as just a God of love. Many people in the Old Testament didn't believe in God's judgment of His people either.

CHANGELESS • God said, "I the Lord do not change" (Mal. 3:6). "Jesus Christ [God] is the same yesterday and today and forever" (Heb. 13:8). We do not serve two Gods—one Old Testament God and one New Testament God. The Lord is One. He doesn't change. Let's look together at the nature of God.

◆ Read the Scriptures at the right and on the next page. Circle words or phrases that tell you something about God.

God is beyond our understanding. Yet God has revealed Himself and His ways in Scripture. God is perfect love. God forever convinced us of His love through the death of Jesus on the cross. God is kind, compassionate, patient, and slow to anger. God is also just. He never punishes the innocent. God's judgments are always right and fair. Yet, God also is merciful. He forgives us when we repent and return to Him.

God is holy and pure. He cannot tolerate our sin. Because of His holiness and justice, God must deal with our sin. God does get angry, and He sometimes displays His wrath on rebellious people. We need to develop a healthy fear of our holy God. When you enter God's presence, you will sense His holiness. You also will see clearly the sin in your life. When a church experiences genuine worship in God's presence, they will realize any sin for which they may need forgiveness.

JONAH 4:2 • I knew that you are a gracious and compassionate God, slow to anger and abounding in love, a God who relents from sending calamity.

1 JOHN 4:8-9 • ⁸God is love. ⁹This is how God showed his love among us: He sent his one and only Son into the world that we might live through him.

NEHEMIAH 9:31 • In your great mercy you did not put an end to them or abandon them, for you are a gracious and merciful God.

JEREMIAH 9:24 • "Let him who boasts boast about this: that he understands and knows me, that I am the Lord, who exercises kindness, justice and righteousness on earth, for in these I delight," declares the Lord.

PSALM 51:4 • Against you, you only, have I sinned and done what is evil in your sight, so that you are proved right when you speak and justified when you judge.

ROMANS 2:5 • Because of your stubbornness and your unrepentant heart, you are storing up wrath against yourself for the day of God's wrath, when his righteous judgment will be revealed.

◆ Read the following Scriptures and see what God takes pleasure in.

EZEKIEL 18:23,32 • [23]"Do I take any pleasure in the death of the wicked? declares the Sovereign Lord. Rather, am I not pleased when they turn from their ways and live?"

[32]"I take no pleasure in the death of anyone, declares the Sovereign Lord. Repent and live!"

2 PETER 3:9 • He is patient with you, not wanting anyone to perish, but everyone to come to repentance.

◆ Which of the following are true about God? Write "T" beside all that are true.

____ a. God delights in the death of wicked people.

____ b. God delights when people turn from wicked ways.

____ c. God wants all people to repent.

____ d. God does not want anyone to perish.

God does not delight in the death of anyone. God wants all people to repent and turn to Him. The last three are true.

◆ Review your memory verses that you have memorized in the past weeks.

Review the seven phases in God's Pattern listed on the inside back cover of this book. See if you can explain the diagram (page 99) through Phase 3.

PSALM 78:38 • Yet he was merciful; he forgave their iniquities and did not destroy them. Time after time he restrained his anger and did not stir up his full wrath.

DANIEL 9:9 • The Lord our God is merciful and forgiving, even though we have rebelled against him.

PSALM 33:4-5 • [4]For the word of the Lord is right and true; he is faithful in all he does. [5]The Lord loves righteousness and justice; the earth is full of his unfailing love.

PSALM 9:7-8 • [7]The Lord reigns forever; he has established his throne for judgment. [8]He will judge the world in righteousness; he will govern the peoples with justice.

ISAIAH 5:16 • But the Lord Almighty will be exalted by his justice, and the holy God will show himself holy by his righteousness.

ISAIAH 30:18 • The Lord longs to be gracious to you; he rises to show you compassion. For the Lord is a God of justice. Blessed are all who wait for him!

ENCOUNTERING GOD IN PRAYER

Read again the traits of God that you have studied today. Take time to thank God for His love, mercy, patience, and kindness. Think about some specific times when God forgave you. Thank Him.

Day 2: God's Purpose in Discipline

A BROKENHEARTED FATHER • God created and called out His people for a love relationship with Himself. When God's people depart from that love relationship, He is grieved. God is brokenhearted over the broken love relationship. Like God did in the Old Testament, He disciplines His people and invites them to return to Him.

◆ Fill in the blanks in Phases 1-2 below.

Phase 1: *God is on _____ to _____ a lost world. He calls His _____ into a relationship with Himself, and He accomplishes His work through them.*

Phase 2: *God's people tend to _____ from _____ turning to substitutes for His _____, _____, and _____.*

Fill in the key words in Phase 3.

Phase 3: *God _____ His people because of His _____.*

God created His people for a love relationship. God knows that fullness of life is found only in that relationship. When we move out of the relationship, God knows we are missing out on the life for which He created us. Because of His love, God disciplines His people when they depart from Him and sin. We need to feel the pain of the lost love relationship so we will return to God.

◆ Read Hebrews 12:5-11.

What three words in verses 5-6 describe what God does to correct His children? R_____, D_____, P_____.

What is true about the person who is not disciplined by the Lord? (v. 8) _____.

HEBREWS 12:5-11 • **⁵You have forgotten that** word of encourage**ment that addresses you** as sons: "My son, do not ma**ke light of the Lord's** disci-pline, and do not lo**se heart when he rebukes you,** ⁶because the Lord di**sciplines those he loves,** and he punishes everyone h**e accepts as a son."** ⁷Endure hardship as disciplin**e; God is treating** you as sons. ⁸If you are not disci**plined . . . you are** illegitimate children and not tru**e sons.** ⁹**Moreover, we** have all had human fathers **who disciplined us and** we respected them for i**t. How much more should** we submit to the Father **of our spirits and live!** ¹⁰. . . God disciplines us fo**r our good, that** we may share in his holiness. ¹¹No **discipline seems** pleasant at the time, but painful. La**ter on, however, it** produces a harvest of righteous**ness and peace** for those who have been trained by **it.**

God's Loving Discipline

⁵Do not **make light of** the Lord's discipline, and do not lose **heart when he** rebukes you, ⁶because the Lord **disciplines those** he loves, and he pun-ishes every**one he accepts** as a son.

—Hebrews 12:5-6

According to verses 10-11, why does God discipline
His children? _____

_____

◆ Begin memorizing Hebrews 12:5-6 about God's
loving discipline.

Human parents discipline their children when they
do wrong. Have you ever said, "This is for your
own good" or "This is going to hurt me more than
it will hurt you"? Parents who love their children
teach them to live correctly.

A LOVING FATHER • God loved us so much that He
sent His Son Jesus to die on a cross for us. Our sin
brought great pain to our Heavenly Father. God
loves us dearly. That is why God rebukes, disciplines, and punishes His children. A person who is
not disciplined is not part of God's family. God's
correction of His children is for their own good.
God wants us to share in His holiness. God wants
us to reap righteousness and peace. Even though
God's discipline may be painful, we should submit
to His correction and live! Notice in verse 5 that
these words should "encourage" you. Be encouraged when you are disciplined by God. That is a
good sign that God loves you.

◆ Why does God discipline His children—His peo-
ple? Check all that apply.
❑ God hates us.
❑ God wants the best in life for us.
❑ God loves us.
❑ God wants to make us miserable.
❑ God wants us to be holy.
❑ God likes to hurt people.

God loves us, and He wants us to be holy. He wants
the best in life for us.

◆ Read the following Scriptures. Circle the words
love and *loved*.

JEREMIAH 31:3 • The Lord appeared to us in the
past, saying: "I have loved you with an everlasting
love; I have drawn you with loving-kindness."

HOSEA 11:4 • "I led them with cords of human
kindness, with ties of love; I lifted the yoke from
their neck and bent down to feed them."

ROMANS 8:35, 37-39 • [35]Who shall separate us from
the love of Christ? Shall trouble or hardship or persecution or famine or nakedness or danger or sword?

[37]No, in all these things we are more than con-
querors through him who loved us. [38]For I am convinced that neither death nor life, neither angels nor
demons, neither the present nor the future, nor any
powers, [39]neither height nor depth, nor anything else
in all creation, will be able to separate us from the
love of God that is in Christ Jesus our Lord.

ENCOUNTERING GOD IN PRAYER

Reflect on the relationship between love and discipline. Pray through the Scriptures above and thank
God for loving and caring about you. Invite God to discipline you anytime He knows you have departed
from Him. Remember, God wants you to experience a more meaningful life with Him.

Day 3: Nature of God's Discipline and Judgment

TEMPORAL AND ETERNAL • Someday soon Jesus is going to return to claim His own people and take them to heaven for eternity. At the end of history God will judge all people. "For we will all stand before God's judgment seat. Each of us will give an account of himself to God" (Rom. 14:10,12). The judgments in the end times will be eternal. Our destiny in heaven or hell will be settled as God separates the "sheep"—his people—from the "goats"—those who do not belong to Him. This unit is not dealing with those judgments, though our responses to God today will affect the outcome of those judgments.

Our primary concern right now is on God's temporal (or earthly) judgments—those that occur in this lifetime. These disciplines and judgments are intended to correct us or to punish us. Because God is loving and patient, His correction almost always comes before punishment. Only after correction fails to bring change does more severe punishment and the wrath of God come. God is sovereign, however. God can do what He pleases. His judgments are always just, fair, and right. God will never give us greater punishment than we deserve.

◆ Write *temporal* and *eternal* beside their definitions.

_____ Rulings that separate God's people to heaven and all others to hell for eternity.
_____ Correction and punishment that occur in this lifetime.

REMEDIAL AND FINAL • There are two types of discipline and judgment in this life. *Remedial* judgments (or discipline) are intended by God to correct

us. They are to guide us back to a right relationship with God. *Final* judgments come when God displays His wrath against sin. When final judgment comes, no opportunity for repentance is left. Time for repentance is past. Final judgments usually come after prolonged periods of sin without repentance. Sometimes God uses a final judgment because the nature of the sin is so great. He uses it at other times because the sin could have great influence in others if He did not deal severely with the sin.

◆ Write *remedial* and *final* beside the correct definitions below.

_____ Discipline or judgment intended to correct us and point us back to a right relationship with God.
_____ Judgment or punishment which ends life because of prolonged rebellion or severe sin.

◆ Read the following two Scriptures. Which type of judgment is described? Write *remedial* or *final* beside the references.

Ananias and Sapphira: Acts 5:1-5_____

Immoral man at Corinth: 1 Corinthians 5:1-2, 4-5,12-13 _____

In this course our focus is on God's remedial discipline or judgment. God's desire is to correct us so that we will return to Him. In the diagram on the inside back cover, the word *judgment* at the bottom is a final judgment in this lifetime. God's desire for His people is that we will never reach that point. Next week we will look at God's call for repentance. The immoral man at Corinth experienced corrective discipline of God carried out by the church. In 2 Corinthians 2:5-11 Paul explained that the correction was effective. Paul asked the church to forgive the man, comfort him, and reaffirm their love for him. The church's correction by Paul also was effective. (See 2 Cor. 7:8-13.)

◆ Read the Scriptures at the right. Beside the Scripture write the letter of the truths listed below.

a. Judgment should begin with the people of God.
b. Every deed, including hidden things, will be judged.
c. God's discipline is progressive. It increases each time we do not respond.
d. Jesus came to bring judgment.

___ JOHN 9:39 • Jesus said, "For judgment I have come into this world."

___ ECCLESIASTES 12:14 • For God will bring every deed into judgment, including every hidden thing, whether it is good or evil.

____ LEVITICUS 26:14,16,18-19,21 • ¹⁴But if you will not listen to me and carry out all these commands,
    ¹⁶then I will do this to you.
    ¹⁸If after all this you will not listen to me, I will punish you for your sins seven times over. ¹⁹I will break down your stubborn pride and . . .
    ²¹If you remain hostile toward me and refuse to listen to me, I will multiply your afflictions seven times over, as your sins deserve.

____ 1 PETER 4:17 • For it is time for judgment to begin with the family of God; and if it begins with us, what will the outcome be for those who do not obey the gospel of God?

(Answers: John 9:39–d; Eccl. 12:14–b; Lev. 26:14,16,18-19,21–c; 1 Pet. 4:17–a)

The Scriptures are filled with examples of God's disciplines and judgments. Some are far more serious than others. As you read yesterday, God's judgments are progressive. They get more severe the longer we refuse personally or corporately to respond.

EXAMPLES OF DISCIPLINE AND JUDGMENT
Natural Disasters: earthquake, volcano, hurricane, tornado, flood, fire, drought, hail, famine, insect plague, attack of wild animals.
Disease: plague, wasting disease, fever, leprosy
Human Conflict or Trouble: war, attack or defeat by an enemy, being taken into captivity, being ruled by those who hate, victim of crime, victim of immorality, bloodshed, increase in wickedness, broken human relationships, economic collapse. (Of course, not all events such as these come from God's discipline and judgment. Scripture records incidences when these events were part of testing as in the case of Job, and persecution as in the early church.)

◆ Read the Scriptures to the right and match them to the descriptions of disciplines of God listed below. Write the reference by one of the descriptions.

Convicts of Sin_____
Refuses to Hear Our Prayers_____
Withdraws His Presence_____
Sends a Famine of His Word_____
Removes His Hedge of Protection_____
Allows the Full Consequences of Sin_____
Destroys or Removes_____

ISAIAH 59:2 • Your iniquities have separated you from your God; your sins have hidden his face from you, so that he will not hear.

REVELATION 2:5 • If you do not repent, I will come to you and remove your lampstand [church] from its place.

AMOS 8:11-12 • [11]"I will send a famine through the land—not a famine of food or a thirst for water, but a famine of hearing the words of the Lord. [12]Men will stagger from sea to sea and wander from north to east, searching for the word of the Lord, but they will not find it."

ISAIAH 5:5 • "I will take away its hedge, and it will be destroyed; I will break down its wall, and it will be trampled."

JEREMIAH 7:13-15 • [13]I spoke to you again and again, but you did not listen; I called you, but you did not answer. [14]Therefore. . . . [15]I will thrust you from my presence.

LUKE 19:43-44 • [43]"The days will come upon you when your enemies will build an embankment against you and encircle you and hem you in on every side. [44]They will dash you to the ground . . . because you did not recognize the time of God's coming to you."

JOHN 16:8 • "He [the Counselor, the Holy Spirit] will convict the world of guilt in regard to sin and righteousness and judgment."

God can discipline us any way He wants. God's desire is that we would respond to the conviction of the Holy Spirit. When we don't judge ourselves and repent, God judges us. God's disciplines will increase until He gets our attention. God does, however, have a limit on His patience. If we continue to refuse to respond, God may bring final judgments. Several final judgments are described in the New Testament. For instance:

• Jesus prophesied the destruction of Jerusalem that took place in A.D. 70. This was a judgment on the Jews for rejecting God. (See Luke 19:11-44.)
• Because of greed, Ananias and Sapphira lied to God about their giving. This planned lie could have infected the early church if not dealt with. They died in a swift and final judgment. (See Acts 5:1-11.)
• Paul rebuked the Corinthian church for not taking the Lord's Supper seriously. People were participating in an unworthy manner. They were sinning against the body and blood of Jesus. Paul said, "That is why many among you are weak and sick, and a number of you have fallen asleep." Some died because they refused to judge themselves properly. (See 1 Cor. 11:17-34.)

Fortunately, God is merciful and patient. God normally gives us many warnings and time to repent. If something "bad" happens to you, how can you know if it is God's discipline? Ask Him. God disciplines you to correct you. If God is disciplining you, He will let you know if you seek an answer. If you *sincerely* seek a word about a "bad" circumstance and you hear nothing from God, you may assume it is not discipline. Discipline is not the only reason for bad events.

ROMANS 1:24-31 • [24]God gave them over in the sinful desires of their hearts to sexual impurity for the degrading of their bodies with one another. [25]They exchanged the truth of God for a lie, and worshiped and served created things rather than the Creator. [26]God gave them over to shameful lusts. Even their women exchanged natural relations for unnatural ones. [27]In the same way the men also abandoned natural relations with women and were inflamed with lust for one another. Men committed indecent acts with other men, and received in themselves the due penalty for their perversion.

[28]He gave them over to a depraved mind, to do what ought not to be done. [29]They have become filled with every kind of wickedness, evil, greed and depravity. They are full of envy, murder, strife, deceit and malice. They are gossips, [30]slanderers, God-haters, insolent, arrogant and boastful; they invent ways of doing evil; they disobey their parents; [31]they are senseless, faithless, heartless, ruthless.

ENCOUNTERING GOD IN PRAYER
Read back through the list of actions God may take to discipline or judge a person, family, or church. Are you experiencing any of these yourself? as a family? as a church? as a town or city? as a nation? If so, ask God if this is His discipline. If it is, repent of the sin He points out to you. Return to God. Pray that the leaders of your church, city, or nation will call the people to return to the Lord.

Day 5: Revival Under Asa and Azariah

Asa, King of Judah, had a heritage of faith. He was the great-great grandson of King David. Asa's father, King Abijah, trusted in the Lord and guided the people to follow the requirements of the Lord. Asa was brought up to trust the Lord and faithfully serve Him. When Asa became king, he "did what was good and right in the eyes of the Lord his God. He removed the foreign altars and the high places. He commanded Judah to seek the Lord, the God of their fathers, and to obey his laws and commands" (2 Chron. 14:2-4). God gave them victory over their enemies. God prospered them. Then, evidently, their hearts departed from the Lord. By chapter 15 of 2 Chronicles, they had been "without the true God" (2 Chron. 15:3). God sent a word to Asa through the prophet Azariah.

◆ Read 2 Chronicles 15:1-7.

In verses 3-6, what problems did God allow in order to discipline His people because of their sin? Underline them. One is underlined as an example. Who was troubling the people with every kind of distress? (v. 6) _____

In verse 2, when did God promise to be with Asa?

_____

What did Asa have to do to find the Lord?

_____

What would God do if Asa forsook the Lord?

_____

God did not overrule the people's choice to forsake Him. God did, however, allow them to suffer the consequences of their sin. The priests were not teaching the law, so the people got further and further away from God. Crime increased so it was not safe to travel about. Nations and cities were at war with each other, and God was troubling the people to get their attention.

King Asa needed this reminder from the Lord. God did not leave Israel; they left Him. God was calling them back into a relationship with Himself. If they would seek the Lord, He would be found. But, if they forsook the Lord, He would forsake them.

2 CHRONICLES 15:1-7 • [1]The Spirit of God came upon Azariah son of Oded. [2]He went out to meet Asa and said to him, "Listen to me, Asa and all Judah and Benjamin. The Lord is with you when you are with him. If you seek him, he will be found by you, but if you forsake him, he will forsake you. [3]For a long time Israel was <u>without the true God</u>, without a priest to teach and without the law. [4]But in their distress they turned to the Lord, the God of Israel, and sought him, and he was found by them. [5]In those days it was not safe to travel about, for all the inhabitants of the lands were in great turmoil. [6]One nation was being crushed by another and one city by another, because God was troubling them with every kind of distress. [7]But as for you, be strong and do not give up, for your work will be rewarded."

> The Lord is with you when you are with him. If you seek him, he will be found by you, but if you forsake him, he will forsake you.
> —2 Chronicles 15:2

◆ Read 2 Chronicles 15:8-15.

What did Asa do to prepare for the return to the Lord? (v. 8) _____

Who assembled to renew the covenant relationship with the Lord? Check one.

❏ The king and key leaders
❏ A representative group of people
❏ All the people living under Asa's rule
❏ Only people interested in attending

Which of the following words describe the way the people sought the Lord? Check all that apply.

❏ reluctantly   ❏ wholeheartedly
❏ eagerly   ❏ with all their heart and soul
❏ quietly   ❏ with shouting
❏ sadly   ❏ with rejoicing

What happened when the people sought the Lord this way? (v. 15) _____

Asa prepared for the return to the Lord by removing the detestable idols and repairing the altar of the Lord. He called all the people together. This was serious business, and the future of the nation depended on the wholehearted response of the people. According to this passage, the people did not come because of pressure from the king. They were not reluctant or sad. They sought the Lord with all their heart and soul. God met His people and restored peace on every side.

Did you see God's pattern for revival? God's people forsook Him. God disciplined them. Then God called them to return to Him. All the people sought God with all their hearts, and He was found. The great joy of revival came after the repentance.

2 CHRONICLES 15:8-15 • ⁸When Asa heard these words and the prophecy of Azariah son of Oded the prophet, he took courage. He removed the detestable idols from the whole land of Judah and Benjamin and from the towns he had captured in the hills of Ephraim. He repaired the altar of the Lord that was in front of the portico of the Lord's temple.

⁹Then he assembled all Judah and Benjamin and the people from Ephraim, Manasseh and Simeon who had settled among them, for large numbers had come over to him from Israel when they saw that the Lord his God was with him.

¹⁰They assembled at Jerusalem . . . ¹¹At that time they sacrificed to the Lord. . . . ¹²They entered into a covenant to seek the Lord, the God of their fathers, with all their heart and soul. ¹³All who would not seek the Lord, the God of Israel, were to be put to death, whether small or great, man or woman. ¹⁴They took an oath to the Lord with loud acclamation, with shouting and with trumpets and horns. ¹⁵All Judah rejoiced about the oath because they had sworn it wholeheartedly. They sought God eagerly, and he was found by them. So the Lord gave them rest on every side.

ENCOUNTERING GOD IN PRAYER

Returning to the Lord may require adjustments, but the results should be joyous. God invites you and your church to return to Him. Ask God to bring your church to a wholehearted desire to seek Him.

Unit 4 Review: God Disciplines His People in Love

◆ As a review of this unit, answer the following questions. If you need help, scan back through the unit for answers.

1. Fill in the blanks in Phase 3 below. Check your answers by referring to the inside back cover.
Phase 3: *God _____ His people out of His _____ for them.*

2. Check each of the following that describes a part of God's nature.

❑ loving, compassionate   ❑ patient, longsuffering
❑ evil, wicked   ❑ just, fair
❑ merciless   ❑ gracious
❑ forgiving   ❑ angry, wrathful
❑ pleased in death of wicked ❑ holy
❑ pure   ❑ righteous

3. Why does God discipline His children, His people?

4. Which of the following words best describes God's corrective discipline?
❑ eternal judgment   ❑ final judgment
❑ remedial judgment

5. List four or five examples of ways God disciplines or judges His people.

6. What statement, Scripture, or idea has been most meaningful to you in this unit?

7. Reword that statement, Scripture, or idea into a prayer response to God.

8. Write from memory Hebrews 12:5-6 describing God's loving discipline.

9. Based on Hebrews 12:5-6 (NIV) what are three things God does to discipline His children in love?

R _____
D _____
P _____

Unit 5: God Calls His People to Repent

When God's people have sinned and they come to Him with a cry for help, God offers two choices: repent or perish. Repentance is required before we can experience the forgiveness and healing of revival. To repent, individuals and churches must change their minds, hearts, and wills. As God's people, we must overcome pride and humble ourselves. We must spend time in prayer and fellowship with God. We must turn from our wicked ways. God requires repentance before He will send revival. God is ready to pour out a spirit of revival on people who return to Him.

DAY 1: "RETURN TO ME"
DAY 2: GOD'S CALL TO REPENTANCE
DAY 3: GOD'S REQUIREMENTS FOR REPENTANCE
DAY 4: CORPORATE REPENTANCE
DAY 5: REVIVAL UNDER JOSIAH AND HILKIAH

LEARNING GOAL

You will understand God's requirements for repentance and demonstrate humility in returning to God.

SCRIPTURE MEMORY VERSE

Malachi 3:7
"Return to me, and I will return to you," says the Lord Almighty.

PHASE 4:
God's people cry out to Him for help.

PHASE 5:
God calls His people to repent and return to Him or perish.

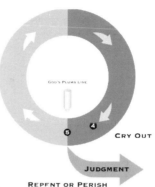

GOD'S PLUMB LINE

CRY OUT

JUDGMENT

REPENT OR PERISH

SUMMARY STATEMENTS

- There is a connection between our sin and what is happening to us.
- God wants His people to return to a love relationship with Him.
- God's discipline indicates a sin problem. Turning to or accepting substitutes for God indicates a spiritual problem. Failure to obey God's commands indicates a problem. These all indicate that our hearts have shifted, that our love relationships with God are not right.
- Sin is serious, and we must treat it as we would a serious wound. We must agree with God that we have done wrong. Repentance requires that we return to our first love. Repentance requires a radical putting away of sin.
- Pride may be the first and greatest barrier to revival.
- God looks not only on our outward actions, He also looks on our hearts.
- After repentance, joy returns to worship.

Prayer Revival of 1857-58

ONE MILLION SAVED • With little human planning, a nation-wide revival broke out among God's people in "union prayer meetings" beginning in 1857. In the awakening that followed, nearly 1,000,000 people accepted Christ and became involved in churches in a two-year period. Based on percentages of converts to the general population, a similar move of God in our day would result in eight or nine million people turning to Christ.

GREAT NEED • The years leading up to 1857 were years of tremendous growth and prosperity for America. Population was booming. People and businesses were becoming wealthy. The "cares of the world" captured the minds and hearts of Americans choking out their interest in God and His kingdom. Churches were declining in numbers, strength, and influence.

UNION PRAYER MEETINGS • The growth of New York City began to force the wealthy residents out of the downtown area. They were replaced by unchurched masses of common laborers. Many churches decided to move to "more fruitful" locations. In a state of decline, the North Dutch Church decided to stay and reach the lost masses around them. They employed a business man, Jeremiah Lanphier, as a lay missionary. He began to visit homes, distribute Bibles and tracts, and advertise church services. Facing a discouraging response, he found comfort in prayer.

One day he prayed, "Lord, what wilt thou have me to do?" He sensed God's leadership to begin a weekly prayer service at the noon hour for workers and business people to commune with God. He began on Wednesday, September 23, 1857, with six people attending. The second week 20 attended, and 40 the third. The hunger and thirst after God was evident, and they began daily "union prayer meetings" the fourth week. People of all classes of society and from many denominations attended.

THE ECONOMIC CRASH OF 1857 • God had a praying people in place when the financial crash of 1857 hit one week after the daily prayer meetings began. "When it [the crash] came, merchants by the thousands all over the country were forced to the wall, banks failed, and railroads went into bankruptcy." In New York City alone 30,000 people lost their jobs. Added to the financial crisis, the nation was gripped by the tensions over slavery. The future of the nation was bleak indeed.

REVIVAL • In the midst of disaster and with a great hunger for God, people flooded the prayer meetings by the thousands. The meetings spread all over town and then across the nation. Businesses even closed to allow their employees time for prayer. The newspapers gave front-page coverage of "Revival News" and revival spread like wildfire across the country. Religion became the common topic of conversation.

AWAKENING • When the revival/awakening was at its peak, 50,000 people were converted every week. Within a year nearly one million people were converted. "Bishop McIlvaine, in his annual address before the Diocesan Convention of Ohio, said: 'I rejoice in the decided conviction that it [the revival/awakening] is "the Lord's doing;" unaccountable by any natural causes, entirely above and beyond what any human device or power could produce; an outpouring of the Spirit of God upon God's people, quickening them to greater earnestness in his service; and upon the unconverted, to make them new creatures in Christ Jesus.'"

Would you be willing to pray, "Lord, what wilt thou have me to do?" Would you be willing to wait on the Lord until He tells you what He wants to do through you for revival in our day? Help your church make prayer a major strategy for revival.

This account has been adapted from *The History of American Revivals* by Frank Grenville Beardsley, 1912 (pp. 213-239). For further reading see *The Fervent Prayer* by J. Edwin Orr, 1974.

Cleansing by Washing with Water Through the Word

> *Christ loved the church and gave himself up for her to make her holy, cleansing her by the washing with water through the word, and to present her to himself as a radiant church, without stain or wrinkle or any other blemish, but holy and blameless.*
> —Ephesians 5:25-27

Read and pray through the following Scriptures this week. Let God speak to you through His Word.

WASH OUT: Are there actions, behaviors, habits, or sins that need to be "washed out" of your life? your family? your church? Confess them (agree with God about the wrong), turn away from them, and turn to God.

WASH IN: Are there good things God wants to "wash into" your life? your family? your church? Pray about those and become all God wants you to be.

HEBREWS 12:1-2 • ¹Therefore, since we are surrounded by such a great cloud of witnesses, let us throw off everything that hinders and the sin that so easily entangles, and let us run with perseverance the race marked out for us. ²Let us fix our eyes on Jesus, the author and perfecter of our faith, who for the joy set before him endured the cross, scorning its shame, and sat down at the right hand of the throne of God.

HEBREWS 12:14-15 • ¹⁴Make every effort to live in peace with all men and to be holy; without holiness no one will see the Lord. ¹⁵See to it that no one misses the grace of God and that no bitter root grows up to cause trouble and defile many.

1 JOHN 3:14 • We know that we have passed from death to life, because we love our brothers. Anyone who does not love remains in death.

PROVERBS 11:19 • The truly righteous man attains life, but he who pursues evil goes to his death.

ACTS 17:29-31 • ²⁹"Since we are God's offspring, we should not think that the divine being is like gold or silver or stone—an image made by man's design and skill. ³⁰In the past God overlooked such ignorance, but now he commands all people everywhere to repent. ³¹For he has set a day when he will judge the world with justice by the man he has appointed. He has given proof of this to all men by raising him from the dead."

MATTHEW 12:41 • "The men of Nineveh will stand up at the judgment with this generation and condemn it; for they repented at the preaching of Jonah, and now one greater than Jonah is here."

EZEKIEL 18:30-32 • ³⁰"Therefore, O house of Israel, I will judge you, each one according to his ways, declares the Sovereign Lord. Repent! Turn away from all your offenses; then sin will not be your downfall. ³¹Rid yourselves of all the offenses you have committed, and get a new heart and a new spirit. Why will you die, O house of Israel? ³²For I take no pleasure in the death of anyone, declares the Sovereign Lord. Repent and live!"

2 CORINTHIANS 6:14-17 • ¹⁴Do not be yoked together with unbelievers. For what do righteousness and wickedness have in common? Or what fellowship can light have with darkness? ¹⁵What harmony is there between Christ and Belial? . . . ¹⁶What agreement is there between the temple of God and idols? . . . ¹⁷"Therefore come out from them and be separate, says the Lord."

LUKE 13:1-5 • ¹Now there were some present at that time who told Jesus about the Galileans whose blood Pilate had mixed with their sacrifices. ²Jesus answered, "Do you think that these Galileans were worse sinners than all the other Galileans because they suffered this way? ³I tell you, no! But unless you repent, you too will all perish."

71

Day 1: "Return to Me"

◆ Fill in the blanks in Phase 3 below. Check your answers on the inside back cover.

Phase 3: *God _____ His people because of His _____.*

◆ Using the inside back cover, fill in the key words in Phases 4 and 5.

Phase 4: *God's people _____ to Him for help.*

Phase 5: *God calls His people to _____ and return to Him or_____.*

GOD'S CALL TO RETURN

"Return to me, and I will return to you," says the Lord Almighty.

—Malachi 3:7

What is God's call to His people in Malachi 3:7?

_____

MAKE THE CONNECTION • When we depart from the Lord, He disciplines us in love. We need to make the connection between our sin and what is happening to us. If we are experiencing God's discipline, we must respond immediately. The longer we delay, the more intense His discipline becomes. God continues to deal with us more severely until He finally gets our attention. Then we cry out to God for help. When we cry out to God, He calls us to repent and return to Him.

King Solomon was the wisest person ever to live. He understood that God's people would sin and depart from Him. As he dedicated the temple, Solomon asked God if He would forgive His people when they cried out to Him.

◆ Read the following verses from 2 Chronicles 6. **What are some of the disciplines or judgments God might bring upon His people?** _____

_____

Why would God bring these disasters upon His people? _____

_____

2 CHRONICLES 6: 24,26,28,36-39

[24] "When your people Israel have been defeated by an enemy because they have sinned.

[26] "When the heavens are shut up and there is no rain because your people have sinned against you.

[28] "When famine or plague comes to the land, or blight or mildew, locusts or grasshoppers, or when enemies besiege them in any of their cities.

[36] "When [Your people] sin against you—for there is no one who does not sin—and you become angry with them and give them over to the enemy, who takes them captive. [37] and if they have a change of heart. [38] and if they turn back to you with all their heart and soul . . . and pray; [39] then from heaven, your dwelling place, hear their prayer and their pleas, and uphold their cause. And forgive your people, who have sinned against you."

God disciplines His people when they sin against Him. Notice that the sin is against God. Solomon knew that God used disasters to punish and correct His people. God used such things as defeat by an enemy, drought, famine, plague, blight, mildew, insect plagues, and captivity to discipline His people. Solomon's question of God was this: "Lord, if You punish Your people because of their sin, and they turn their hearts back to You, will you forgive them?"

◆ Read God's response to Solomon's prayer. Circle the four things God expects from His people and underline what God promises to do in response.

[13]"When I shut up the heavens so that there is no rain, or command locusts to devour the land or send a plague among my people, [14]if my people, who are called by my name, will humble themselves and pray and seek my face and turn from their wicked ways, then will I hear from heaven and will forgive their sin and will heal their land.
— **2 Chronicles 7:13-14**

FOUR REQUIREMENTS FOR REVIVAL
1. Humble yourselves
2. Pray
3. Seek God's face
4. Turn from your wicked ways

GOD'S PROMISE • In essence God answered, "Yes! If I punish my people and they return to Me, I will forgive them and heal their land." In this passage God identified four requirements for revival: God wants His people to return to a love relationship with Him. He wants His people to spend time with Him in prayer. God wants them to seek His presence (His face). God wants them to repent of their wicked ways. Then God will forgive and heal!

◆ Read the following statements of God's call to His people and encounter God in prayer.

JAMES 4:8 • Come near to God and he will come near to you. Wash your hands, you sinners, and purify your hearts, you double-minded.

REVELATION 2:4-5 • [4]You have forsaken your first love. [5]Remember the height from which you have fallen! Repent and do the things you did at first.

REVELATION 3:1-3 • [1]I know your deeds; you have a reputation of being alive, but you are dead. [2]Wake up! Strengthen what remains and is about to die. . . . [3]Remember, therefore, what you have received and heard; obey it, and repent.

REVELATION 3:15-16,19-20 • [15]I know your deeds, that you are neither cold nor hot. . . . [16]Because you are lukewarm . . . I am about to spit you out of my mouth.

[19]Those whom I love I rebuke and discipline. So be earnest, and repent. [20]Here I am! I stand at the door and knock. If anyone hears my voice and opens the door, I will come in and eat with him, and he with me.

ENCOUNTERING GOD IN PRAYER
Is God disciplining you? your family? your church? your town or city? your nation? Hear His voice. Open the door and invite God in for fellowship. Repent and return to your love relationship with God.

Day 2: God's Call to Repentance

SYMPTOMS OF THE PROBLEM • When you go to a doctor with an illness, he examines you looking for symptoms of the illness. Once he sees what the illness is doing to you, he often knows what the cause is. Then he knows how to treat it.

Suppose that your child has a fever and complains of an earache. You take her to the doctor. He finds that her temperature is 102 degrees. She has a high white blood count. Her right ear is red. Everything else seems to be okay. These symptoms are not the primary problem. An ear infection is the problem. The doctor could give aspirin for the fever and the earache but not solve the problem. Your daughter needs an antibiotic to kill the infection.

In a similar way, we can observe symptoms of spiritual illness. The symptoms are not the primary problem. We have already identified three symptoms of spiritual sickness: (1) God's discipline indicates a sin problem. (2) Turning to or accepting substitutes for God indicates a spiritual problem. (3) Disobedience or failure to obey God's commands indicates a problem.

◆ Based on our previous study, what do all three of these symptoms indicate?_____

_____

Yes. These all indicate that our hearts have shifted, that our love relationships with God are not right. Once you see the symptoms in your life, family, church, community, or nation, you need to cry out to God for help. You cannot fix the problem by yourself. The good news is that God has the help

you need. In fact, by the time you respond to His call, God already has everything planned for revival. When God took Israel into captivity because of their sin, He sent a message through Jeremiah. God took the initiative to call His people back to Himself.

JEREMIAH 29:4, 11-14 • ⁴This is what the Lord Almighty, the God of Israel, says to all those I carried into exile from Jerusalem to Babylon. ¹¹"I know the plans I have for you," declares the Lord, "plans to prosper you and not to harm you, plans to give you hope and a future. ¹²Then you will call upon me and come and pray to me, and I will listen to you. ¹³You will seek me and find me when you seek me with all your heart. ¹⁴I will be found by you," declares the Lord, "and will bring you back from captivity."

DEUTERONOMY 30:19-20 • ¹⁹This day I call heaven and earth as witnesses against you that I have set before you life and death, blessings and curses. Now choose life, so that you and your children may live ²⁰and that you may love the Lord your God, listen to his voice, and hold fast to him. For the Lord is your life.

REVELATION 2:5 • Repent and do the things you did at first. If you do not repent, I will come to you and remove your lampstand from its place.

◆ Read Jeremiah 29:4,11-14.

What kind of plans did God have for His people? Check all that apply.

❑ Plans to harm them   ❑ Plans to give hope
❑ Plans to prosper them   ❑ Plans to discourage them

In verse 12 what did God tell the people they would do to begin the return to Him? _____

_____

What was God's promise to His people in verses 13-14? _____

_____

Even when He brought great disaster on His people, God had all the plans in place to bring them back to Himself. God was ready to prosper them and give them hope. God was standing ready for their call to Him in prayer. When they began to seek Him, God would respond to their plea.

◆ Read Deuteronomy 30:19-20 and Revelation 2:5.

Which of the following best describes God's call to His people? Check one.

❑ "Don't worry about our broken love relationship. I'll bless you anyway."
❑ "If you don't want to come back to me with your whole heart, I'll settle for 75 percent."
❑ "Repent and live, or keep going the way you are going and die."

❑ "If you won't accept my terms for revival, I'll bring revival on your terms."

◆ Read the Scriptures below. **Does the New Testament also emphasize repentance?**
❑ Yes   ❑ No

MATTHEW 3:1-2 • [1]In those days John the Baptist came, preaching in the Desert of Judea [2]and saying, "Repent, for the kingdom of heaven is near."

MATTHEW 4:17 • From that time on Jesus began to preach, "Repent, for the kingdom of heaven is near."

MATTHEW 11:20-22 • [20]Jesus began to denounce the cities in which most of his miracles had been performed, because they did not repent. [21]"Woe to you, Korazin! Woe to you, Bethsaida! If the miracles that were performed in you had been performed in Tyre and Sidon, they would have repented long ago in sackcloth and ashes. [22]But I tell you, it will be more bearable for Tyre and Sidon on the day of judgment than for you."

MARK 1:14-15 • [14]Jesus went into Galilee, proclaiming the good news of God. [15]"The time has come," he said. "The kingdom of God is near. Repent and believe the good news!"

1 JOHN 1:9 • If we confess our sins, he is faithful and just and will forgive us our sins and purify us from all unrighteousness.

ENCOUNTERING GOD IN PRAYER

Do you sense a need for revival? Have you seen symptoms of a spiritual problem in your life, family, church, city, or nation? God already has everything in place to bring about revival. God is waiting for the response of His people. Spend some time responding to God right now.

Day 3: God's Requirements for Repentance

God calls His people to repent or perish. Sin is serious, and we must treat it as we would a serious wound (see Jer. 6:13-14,16). God does not, however, let us set the conditions of repentance. Repentance does not mean being sorry that you were caught. It is not just feeling sorrow for your sin. Repentance is not taking an action to get away from God's wrath.

The word *repent* indicates turning away from our sin and returning with our whole heart to a love relationship with God. Sorrow is not enough. Reforming our behavior for a while is not enough. Returning to some religious activity is not enough. God wants us to love Him with all our hearts. When we return to the love relationship with Him, the actions of our lives will reflect the change.

◆ Read Luke 3:3,7-8.

Which comes first? (v. 3)
Circle one: forgiveness   repentance

Which of the following shows real repentance? (v. 8) Check one.
- ❑ Saying I'm sorry.
- ❑ Being baptized to clean away my sin.
- ❑ Living my life in a way that shows a change of heart and life-style.

Repentance comes before forgiveness. Sorrow for sin is not enough. "Godly sorrow brings repentance that leads to salvation. . . but worldly sorrow brings death" (2 Cor. 7:10). Broken hearts over our sin lead us to repent. Our hearts and life-styles will change showing that we have repented. Paul explained how new life in Christ reflects repentance in Galatians 2:20. Once we die to self, Christ takes up residence in our lives. He becomes our life. He lives through us. We show genuine repentance by letting Christ live through us. Repentance for God's people—individuals and churches—involves a change in four areas.

JEREMIAH 6:13-14,16 • [13]"Prophets and priests alike, all practice deceit. [14]They dress the wound of my people as though it were not serious. 'Peace, peace,' they say, when there is no peace."
[16]This is what the Lord says: "Stand at the crossroads and look; ask for the ancient paths, ask where the good way is, and walk in it, and you will find rest for your souls."

LUKE 3:3,7-8 • [3]He went into all the country around the Jordan, preaching a baptism of repentance for the forgiveness of sins.
[7]John said to the crowds coming out to be baptized by him, "You brood of vipers! Who warned you to flee from the coming wrath? [8]Produce fruit in keeping with repentance."

GALATIANS 2:20 • I have been crucified with Christ and I no longer live, but Christ lives in me. The life I live in the body, I live by faith in the Son of God, who loved me and gave himself for me."

JEREMIAH 31:27-28 • [27]"The days are coming," declares the Lord, "when I will plant the house of Israel and the house of Judah with the offspring of men and of animals. [28]Just as I watched over them to uproot and tear down, and to overthrow, destroy and bring disaster, so I will watch over them to build and to plant," declares the Lord.

1. Change Your Mind. The first change required is a change of mind. We must agree with God about the truth. We must agree that what we have done is wrong. If we want to argue with God about whether we have done wrong, we haven't yet repented. If we try to give God excuses to justify ourselves, we haven't yet repented. We must come to say like David, "Against you, you only, have I sinned and done what is evil in your sight" (Ps. 51:4).

◆ What is one change required in repentance?

_____

2. Change Your Heart. We must see how we have broken the heart of our Heavenly Father because of our sin. Do you realize that Jesus had to die on the cross to forgive you of your sin? Instead of enjoying our sinful ways, we must come to the place that we grieve over our sin. David said, "The sacrifices of God are a broken spirit; a broken and contrite heart, O God, you will not despise" (Ps. 51:17). We begin our departure from God when we have a shift of our hearts –when we leave our first love. Repentance requires that we return to our first love. We must have a change of heart.

3. Change Your Will. Repentance requires a turning away from the sin. We flirt with temptation when we should flee from it. Repentance requires radically putting away our sin—radical surgery. We must get rid of any idol of the heart, tear down any stronghold, and remove ourselves from tempting situations. That requires a change of our will. If you desire to change your will, God will enable you to do so: "for it is God who works in you to will and to act according to his good purpose" (Phil. 2:13). God even helps in the surgery (see Jer. 31:27-28).

◆ What are two more changes required in repentance? _____ _____

_____

4. Change Your Actions. Repentance requires returning to God's way of living. This requires a new way of living. If your love relationship is right, you will obey Him. Repentance is complete when you bear the fruit (signs) of repentance in a new way of living.

◆ What is a fourth change required in repentance?_____

Day 4: Corporate Repentance

REQUIRED • Whenever people depart from God and sin, repentance is required. This not only includes individuals but also families, committees, churches, denominations, Christian organizations, businesses, cities, nations.

When a group or church repents, we call that *corporate* repentance.

All sin is serious. Sin cannot be dealt with lightly. God condemned the spiritual leaders of Judah because they dressed the wound (sin and rebellion) of His people as if it were not serious. (See Jer. 6:14.) We cannot just forget about sin or hide it for fear of causing problems with others or for fear of harming our reputations. Corporate (group) repentance is required for corporate sin. Without repentance there is no forgiveness. Without forgiveness we cannot return to God.

◆ Read the messages of the Risen Christ to the five churches in Revelation 2—3:
   REVELATION 2:1,4-5
   REVELATION 2:12,14-16
   REVELATION 2:18,20-23
   REVELATION 3:1-3
   REVELATION 3:14-20

To whom was Christ speaking in each case?

_____

Were these messages for individuals or churches?

_____

_____

What common message do all five of these letters contain?_____

An angel is a messenger. Some have considered the angels in Revelation 2—3 to be the pastors of the churches—messengers of God to His people. Whether or not they are the pastors, the messages were intended for the churches. The common thread in all five of the messages is a call to repentance. Churches can sin, and God calls churches to repent. The refusal to repent can be fatal to individuals as well as churches. How does a church or other religious group repent?

Second Chronicles 7:14 was spoken by God to His people. For revival to come and the land be healed, God's people must humble themselves. Pride may be the first and greatest barrier to revival. Because of our pride, churches do not want to admit that they have done anything wrong. They certainly don't want to do it publicly. If cover ups can get a politician in trouble, how do you think God responds when His people try to cover up their sin? We must first forget our pride and humble ourselves before God.

◆ What is the first and perhaps greatest barrier to revival?
_____

After humility comes prayer—communicating with God and seeking His presence. Hiding from God is no good. Trying to run from God or avoid Him cannot help. We must seek God, return to Him, come near to Him, and talk with Him. God said to Judah, "Come now, let us reason together. Though your sins are like scarlet, they shall be as white as snow; though they are red as crimson, they shall be like wool" (Isa. 1:18).

◆ What are three requirements for corporate repentance?
1. Humble ourselves
2. _____ 3. _____

Then we must turn from our wicked ways. Repentance requires a change in mind, heart, and will. When repentance has occurred, the fruit of repentance will be seen in a new way of living according to God's standards. A church must agree with God about the nature of sin. A broken and contrite heart with a wholehearted desire to return to the Lord must be demonstrated. A church must turn away from sin to complete repentance. This may require tearing down "idols," changing the way we do things, getting rid of traditions, selling property or material things, making restitution for a wrong committed, reconciling with others, and accepting those God has accepted. Saying, "We'll just try to do better next time" is not enough. Repentance requires actions that demonstrate a new way of life in the present, not a promise for the future.

◆ What is a fourth requirement for repentance?
1. Humble ourselves   3. Seek God's face
2. Pray   4. _____

2 CHRONICLES 7:14 • "If my people, who are called by my name, will humble themselves and pray and seek my face and turn from their wicked ways, then will I hear from heaven and will forgive their sin and will heal their land."

ENCOUNTERING GOD IN PRAYER

Ask God to guide you as you prayerfully consider these questions. Can you pinpoint ways your church has departed from God and turned to substitutes for Him? Has your church ever willingly disobeyed God? Has God's forgiveness been experienced in your church? Does it need to be?

Day 5: Revival Under Josiah and Hilkiah

In the eighteenth year of King Josiah's reign, he began to repair the temple of the Lord. While cleaning the temple, Hilkiah the priest found the book of the Law. When Josiah heard the Law read, he looked at all they were doing as a nation in light of God's law—His plumb line. Josiah cried out to God. He tore his robes in brokenness before God and said: "Great is the Lord's anger that is poured out on us because our fathers have not kept the word of the Lord; they have not acted in accordance with all that is written in this book" (2 Chron. 34:21). Josiah sought a word from the Lord through the prophetess Huldah. She sought the Lord and brought back a word from Him.

◆ In 2 Chronicles 34:21 Josiah was fearful. Who had not kept the word of the Lord? _____

_____

In your Bible, continue in 2 Chronicles 34. Read verses 24 and 25. What was God planning to do because of the sins of His people?

_____

SINS OF THE FATHERS • Because of the sins of previous generations, the temple was in shambles. The book of the Law had been lost. King Josiah did not even know the requirements of the Lord until the book was read to him. He was fearful because He now knew that God had promised to punish His people if they did not keep His covenant and His Law. Josiah must have felt betrayed by his fathers who were kings before him. "How could they be so irresponsible?" he must have asked. Josiah saw

clearly the symptoms of a people who had departed from the Lord. As leader, he immediately went to the Lord for directions.

TOO LATE FOR THE NATION • First God told Josiah it was too late. His final judgment was going to come on the nation. God is very patient, but He does not withhold His anger forever. About 40 years later, God told Jeremiah: "Do not pray for the well-being of this people. Although they fast, I will not listen to their cry; though they offer burnt offerings and grain offerings, I will not accept them. Instead, I will destroy them with the sword, famine and plague" (Jer. 14:11-12).

God's call to His people is "repent or perish." When we hear that call, we need to respond. The time will come when repentance is no longer an option. At that point our only expectation is judgment. Fortunately for Josiah, God saw his brokenness and delayed sending judgment.

◆ Read 2 Chronicles 34:27-28 and write below what Josiah did that pleased God.

_____

_____

_____

_____

A GENERATION SAVED • God doesn't just look on our outward actions. God looks on our hearts. God saw that Josiah truly was brokenhearted because of the sins of the people. His response saved a whole generation from God's final judgment. Josiah guided the people as they all returned to the Lord.

◆ Read 2 Chronicles 34:29-33.

Whom did Josiah call together in the assembly before God?_____ _____

What did Josiah do or guide the people to do in returning to the Lord? Number from 1 to 5 the following events in the order in which they occurred.

____ Pledged to obey God.
____ Renewed their covenant relationship with God with all their heart.
____ Read God's Word in the hearing of all the leaders and the people.
_ __ Followed the Lord God as long as Josiah lived.
____ Removed all the false gods that the people had been worshiping.

Josiah guided the people to repent. Josiah read God's Word in the hearing of all the leaders and the people. They renewed their covenant relationship with God. They pledged to obey God. They gave evidence of their return to the Lord by removing all the false gods. They followed the Lord with all their hearts. Once the people had repented, Josiah guided the people in the celebration of the Passover and the Feast of Unleavened Bread. This was a time of celebration and praise for all the things God had done for Israel in delivering the people from Egyptian bondage. After repentance, joy returned to worship: "The Passover had not been observed like this in Israel since the days of the prophet Samuel" (2 Chron. 35:18).

ENCOUNTERING GOD IN PRAYER

Begin to pray to the Lord for your church. Pray that the church will do all that God requires to experience revival. Pray especially for your pastor as he leads God's people.

Unit 5 Review: God Calls His People to Repent

◆ As a review of this unit, answer the following questions. If you need help, scan back through the unit for answers.

1. Fill in the blanks in Phases 4 and 5 below. Check your answers by looking at the inside back cover.

Phase 4: *God's people* _____ *to Him for help.*

Phase 5: *God calls His people to* _____ *and return to Him or* _____.

2. What are God's four requirements for revival?
1. _____ 3. _____
2. _____ 4. _____

3. Define *repent* **in your own words.**

_____
_____
_____

4. What are three changes required in repentance?
*Change in:*_____
*Change in:*_____
*Change in:*_____

5. What statement, Scripture, or idea has been most meaningful to you in this unit?_____

_____
_____
_____
_____

6. Reword that statement, Scripture, or idea into a prayer response to God._____

_____
_____
_____
_____
_____

7. Write from memory Malachi 3:7 describing God's call to return._____

_____
_____
_____
_____
_____

Unit 6: God Revives His Repentant People

UNIT OVERVIEW

Revival is a work of Sovereign God. God initiates revival and brings it about when His people repent. When God revives His people, God affirms them for His glory. God exalts His Son Jesus before a watching world. God draws people to Himself. After revival, God brings spiritual awakening.

DAY 1: GOD'S STRATEGY TO WIN A LOST WORLD

DAY 2: REVIVAL UNDER HEZEKIAH

DAY 3: REVIVAL IN THE CHURCH

DAY 4: REVIVAL IS GOD'S WORK

DAY 5: PREPARING THE WAY OF THE LORD

LEARNING GOAL

You will understand God's role in revival and demonstrate a commitment to prepare the way for the Lord to come in revival and awakening.

SCRIPTURE MEMORY VERSE

Ephesians 3:20-21
[20]To him who is able to do immeasurably more than all we ask or imagine, according to his power that is at work within us, [21]to him be glory in the church in Christ Jesus throughout all generations, for ever and ever! Amen.

PHASE 6:

God revives His repentant people by restoring them to a right relationship with Himself.

PHASE 7:

God exalts His Son Jesus in His people and draws the lost to saving faith in Him.

SUMMARY STATEMENTS

- God wants to take the lives that He has redeemed and affirm them for His glory.
- When God comes in revival, He comes as a refiner's fire. God burns away the impurities.
- Individuals and churches cannot continue to do business as usual when God is calling them to revival.
- Prayer is not just a religious activity. Prayer is a relationship between a person and God.
- Repentance is the ultimate requirement. Without repentance, no revival will take place.
- The way to know if we have returned is to see if God has returned to us.
- Revival has not taken place unless a change of heart has taken place.
- Spiritual awakening is a by-product of God's people getting their hearts right with Him.

Asbury Revival

A 185-HOUR CHAPEL SERVICE • Asbury College and Asbury Theological Seminary are located in Wilmore, Kentucky, near Lexington. In 1970 when other college campuses across the nation were filled with strife and protests, these campuses experienced a fresh encounter with God. During the college's regular chapel service on Tuesday, February 3, God brought a fresh wind of His Spirit upon the students. The testimonies, singing, confessing of sin, and praying that began that Tuesday morning continued uninterrupted for 185 hours and ended about 3:00 a.m. Wednesday—more than a week later.

When a God-sent revival breaks out during a time of spiritual hunger, like the days of 1970, it cannot be contained. The testimonies of those present began to spread the refining fires of repentance and revival, first to the adjacent seminary and then to churches and campuses across the nation. The Asbury Revival illustrates the way God uses a person's personal testimony of a divine encounter to stir the hearts of other believers.

The dean felt led to guide a time of testimony that Tuesday morning. He began by sharing his own testimony of faith and then encouraged others to do so.

One senior shocked the audience by confessing, "I'm not believing that I'm standing here telling you what God has done for me. I've wasted my time in college up to now, but Christ has met me and I'm different. Last night the Holy Spirit flooded in and filled my life. Now, for the first time ever, I am excited about being a Christian! I wouldn't want to go back to the emptiness of yesterday for anything."

The testimonies became real, fervent, up-to-date reports of God's activity. Toward the end of the chapel service an invitation was opened for students who wanted to come to the altar for prayer and renewal of their commitment to Christ. A flood of students responded. Then came confessions of theft, cheating, resentment, jealousy, lust, worldly attitudes, prejudice, pride, hatred, and a variety of other sins. Students sought forgiveness. Broken relationships were reconciled. Some made restitution for sins committed. Many in the auditorium had an awesome sense of God's presence.

REVIVAL SPREAD BY WORD OF MOUTH • Word about the revival began to spread by phone, news reports, and word of mouth. Before long visitors began to arrive to experience the revival first hand. They carried the testimony of God's activity back to their churches and campuses where revival often followed. Witnessing teams of students carried the testimony to churches, and 130 colleges, seminaries, and Bible schools across the nation were touched by the revival outreach.

Church, denominational, and racial barriers were demolished by the Holy Spirit. In some cases whole towns were swept up in the revival. In the high school in South Pittsburg, Tennessee, 500 of the 700 students made commitments to Jesus Christ. People responded to God's call to missions and church-related vocations. By the end of 1970 the testimony of God's mighty activity had been shared across North America and on four other continents of the world.

A SHORT LIFE • After the Asbury Revival many anticipated that God was in the process of sending another great awakening. Though the revival was widespread, it was short lived. One possible reason for this short life is that the revival was primarily experience oriented rather than Word-centered. Experience and emotional response to God can only carry you so far. The deep and long lasting revivals in history have been Word-centered revivals. As people return to God and His plumb line, lives, churches, cities, and whole nations have experienced deep and lasting change.

This account has been adapted from *One Divine Moment: The Asbury Revival* edited by Robert E. Coleman, Old Tappan: Fleming H. Revell Company, 1970.

Cleansing by Washing with Water Through the Word

> *Christ loved the church and gave himself up for her to make her holy, cleansing her by the washing with water through the word, and to present her to himself as a radiant church, without stain or wrinkle or any other blemish, but holy and blameless.*
> —Ephesians 5:25-27

Read the following Scriptures and let God speak to you. Use arrows to mark items to "wash out" or "wash in" to your life.

WASH OUT: Are there actions, behaviors, habits, or sins that need to be "washed out" of your life? family? or church?

WASH IN: Are there good things God wants to "wash into" your life? your family? your church?

2 TIMOTHY 2:22-23 • [22]Flee the evil desires of youth, and pursue righteousness, faith, love and peace, along with those who call on the Lord out of a pure heart. [23]Don't have anything to do with foolish and stupid arguments, because you know they produce quarrels.

PHILIPPIANS 2:1-2 • [1]If you have any encouragement from being united with Christ, if any comfort from his love, if any fellowship with the Spirit, if any tenderness and compassion, [2]then make my joy complete by being like-minded, having the same love, being one in spirit and purpose.

EPHESIANS 4:2-3 • [2]Be completely humble and gentle; be patient, bearing with one another in love. [3]Make every effort to keep the unity of the Spirit through the bond of peace.

GALATIANS 6:7-8 • [7]Do not be deceived: God cannot be mocked. A man reaps what he sows. [8]The one who sows to please his sinful nature, from that nature will reap destruction; the one who sows to please the Spirit, from the Spirit will reap eternal life.

1 CORINTHIANS 13:4-8 • [4]Love is patient, love is kind. It does not envy, it does not boast, it is not proud. [5]It is not rude, it is not self-seeking, it is not easily angered, it keeps no record of wrongs. [6]Love does not delight in evil but rejoices with the truth. [7]It always protects, always trusts, always hopes, always perseveres. [8]Love never fails.

JOHN 12:31-32 • [31]"Now is the time for judgment on this world; now the prince of this world will be driven out. [32]But I, when I am lifted up from the earth, will draw all men to myself."

MATTHEW 9:37-38 • [37]"The harvest is plentiful but the workers are few. [38]Ask the Lord of the harvest, therefore, to send out workers into his harvest field."

PHILIPPIANS 2:14-16 • [14]Do everything without complaining or arguing, [15]so that you may become blameless and pure, children of God without fault in a crooked and depraved generation, in which you shine like stars in the universe [16]as you hold out the word of life.

1 PETER 3:15 • In your hearts set apart Christ as Lord. Always be prepared to give an answer to everyone who asks you to give the reason for the hope that you have. But do this with gentleness and respect.

2 CORINTHIANS 3:18 • We, who with unveiled faces all reflect the Lord's glory, are being transformed into his likeness with ever-increasing glory, which comes from the Lord.

ROMANS 13:11-12,14 • [11]The hour has come for you to wake up from your slumber, because our salvation is nearer now than when we first believed. [12]The night is nearly over; the day is almost here. So let us put aside the deeds of darkness and put on the armor of light.

[14]Clothe yourselves with the Lord Jesus Christ, and do not think about how to gratify the desires of the sinful nature.

Day 1: God's Strategy to Win a Lost World

◆ As you begin today's study, open this book to the inside back cover. Refresh your memory by reading through the Seven Phases of God's Pattern.

Fill in the blanks in Phases 4-7.

Phase 4: *God's people _____ to Him for help.*
Phase 5: *God calls His people to_____ and return to Him or _____.*
Phase 6: *God _____ His repentant people by restoring them to a _____ relationship with _____.*
Phase 7: *God exalts His Son _____ in His people and draws the lost to saving _____ in Him.*

What is God's method to win a lost world back to Himself? Certainly the cross, the resurrection, and Pentecost form the centerpiece of His plan. When that work was accomplished by Jesus, how did God intend to touch the rest of the world for the rest of the ages? God called out a people and radically saved them through the death and resurrection of His Son. God forgave them of their sin and made a new creation. God filled them with His presence (Holy Spirit) and power to do His will.

God wants to take the lives that He has redeemed and put them on display. Then the whole world, even the principalities and powers in the heavenly places, might know the wisdom and power of God (see Eph. 3:10-11). How will He do it? Through the church.

GOD'S GLORY IN THE CHURCH

[20]To him who is able to do immeasurably more than all we ask or imagine, according to his power that is at work within us, [21]to him be glory in the church and in Christ Jesus throughout all generations, for ever and ever!
—Ephesians 3:20-21

◆ Read and begin memorizing Ephesians 3:20-21. How much is God able to do?

Whose power accomplishes God's work through His churches? Check one.
❏ Our power   ❏ God's power

Where does God get glory? Fill in the blanks: *To him be glory in the_____ in Christ _____.*

God has called out a people to be on mission with Him. A call to salvation is a call to be on mission with Him. When a person comes to Christ as Savior and Lord, God adds that person to a church—a specific body of Christ. (See 1 Cor. 12:18,27.) When God has members of a church rightly related to Himself and to each other, He is able to exalt His Son Jesus through them. God's power, not ours, is at work in the church to do far more than we could even dream or ask for. He works it to redeem a lost world and bring glory to Himself. God is glorified through Christ Jesus in His church.

◆ Read the Scriptures listed and answer the questions about our role in God's plan.

Second Corinthians 2:14-15—What does God spread everywhere through us? Underline your answer.
Second Corinthians 3:18—What are we to reflect to a watching world? Underline your answer.
Second Corinthians 4:1-2,5-7—Where does this glory and power come from? Check one. *The glory and power comes from...* ❏ us ❏ God
Second Corinthians 5:18-20—What ministry has God given us? Underline it.

When Jesus is magnified in the church, God draws people to saving faith in His Son. God has chosen to reveal His Son Jesus through the churches so that He may reconcile the world to Himself.

When the people of God return to Him, God brings revival. *Revival* means the return of life and vitality. Only God, however, can give renewed life—God is our life. So, God brings revival to His people. When the people of God have returned to God on His terms, then once again the mighty presence of God lifts His people into the middle of His activity. Then God mightily works to touch a lost world. That is what we call spiritual awakening.

2 CORINTHIANS 2:14-15 • [14]Thanks be to God, who always leads us in triumphal procession in Christ and through us spreads everywhere the fragrance of the knowledge of him. [15]For we are to God the aroma of Christ among those who are being saved.

2 CORINTHIANS 3:18 • [18]We, who ... all reflect the Lord's glory, are being transformed into his likeness with ever-increasing glory, which comes from the Lord.

2 CORINTHIANS 4:1-2,5-7 • [1]Since through God's mercy we have this ministry ... [2]we have renounced secret and shameful ways ... [5]we do not preach ourselves, but Jesus Christ as Lord. . . . [6]For God ... made his light shine in our hearts to give us the light of the knowledge of the glory of God in the face of Christ. [7]But we have this treasure in jars of clay to show that this all-surpassing power is from God and not from us.

2 CORINTHIANS 5:18-20 • [18]God ... reconciled us to himself through Christ and gave us the ministry of reconciliation: [19]that God was reconciling the world to himself in Christ. . . . And he has committed to us the message of reconciliation. [20]We are therefore Christ's ambassadors, as though God were making his appeal through us.

ENCOUNTERING GOD IN PRAYER
Thank God for the work He has done in your life and in your church that reflects His power and glory. If you sense that your church needs revival, pray the following biblical prayer for revival:
PSALM 85:4-7 • [4]Restore us again, O God our Savior, and put away your displeasure toward us. [5] Will you be angry with us forever? . . . [6]Will you not revive us again that your people may rejoice in you? [7]Show us your unfailing love, O Lord.

Day 2: Revival Under Hezekiah

THE NATION HAD BEEN LED INTO IDOLATRY •
Ahaz was a wicked king who shut up the temple of
the Lord and worshiped other gods openly. He even
sacrificed some of his own sons by fire. Because of
his wickedness, "the Lord his God handed him over
to the king of Aram. . . . He was also given into the
hands of the king of Israel" (2 Chron. 28:5). The
nation reached a low point spiritually under Ahaz's
leadership. Hezekiah, his son, became king of Judah
following the sixteen-year reign of Ahaz. He did not
follow the pattern of his father Ahaz.

◆ Read 2 Chronicles 29:1-6,8-10.
**What did Hezekiah do (v. 3) and what did he ask the
Levites to do (v. 5) to get ready for revival?**

_____

_____

**Of the seven phases in God's pattern for revival,
which one do you see described . . .**

in verse 6?	_Phase_ ____
in verses 8-9?	_Phase_ ____
in verse 10?	_Phase_ ____

GETTING READY FOR REVIVAL • A wise spiritual
leader will recognize the symptoms of spiritual sickness in the people of God. Hezekiah knew that their
fathers had forsaken the Lord (Phase 2, v. 6). He saw
the destruction, death, and captivity of Judah and
Jerusalem as God's judgments on His people for their
sin (Phase 3, vv. 8-9). Hezekiah knew that it was time
to cry out to the Lord (Phase 4, v. 10). To prepare for
revival, Hezekiah had the place of worship repaired,

cleansed, and dedicated to the Lord once again.
The spiritual leaders (Levites) spent 16 days consecrat-
ing the temple and removing all the unclean things.
Hezekiah then gathered all the city officials and they
went to the temple to offer sacrifices to the Lord. The
temple musicians were called to assist with the worship. "So the service of the temple of the Lord was
reestablished. Hezekiah and all the people rejoiced at
what God had brought about for his people, because
it was done so quickly" (2 Chron. 29:35-36).

2 CHRONICLES 29:1-6,8-10 • [1]Hezekiah . . . [2]did
what was right in the eyes of the Lord. . . . [3]In the
first month of the first year of his reign, he opened
the doors of the temple of the Lord and repaired
them. [4]He brought in the priests and the Levites . . .
[5]and said: "Listen to me, Levites! Consecrate yourselves now and consecrate the temple of the Lord,
the God of your fathers. Remove all defilement
from the sanctuary. [6]Our fathers were unfaithful;
they did evil in the eyes of the Lord our God and
forsook him.

[8]Therefore, the anger of the Lord has fallen on
Judah and Jerusalem; he has made them an object
of dread and horror and scorn, as you can see with
your own eyes. [9]This is why our fathers have fallen
by the sword and why our sons and daughters and
our wives are in captivity. [10]Now I intend to make a
covenant with the Lord, the God of Israel, so that
his fierce anger will turn away from us.

A CALL TO WORSHIP • Hezekiah sent word to all Israel and Judah to assemble for the Passover celebration. The time had already passed for the celebration, but the leaders sensed that they could not wait another year.

◆ In your Bible, read the call to worship in 2 Chronicles 30:6-9.

Write a title that best summarizes the passage.

_____

Underline the promise in verse 9. What must the people do? _____

_____

Hezekiah called the people to return to the Lord. This was a call to worship. Not everyone wanted to return to the Lord. They scorned and ridiculed the messengers. Others, however, humbled themselves and gathered to worship. And "the hand of God was on the people to give them unity of mind to carry out what the king and his officials had ordered" (2 Chron. 30:12).

◆ As you read the following, circle the signs that revival had taken place.

REVIVAL AND THE FRUIT OF REPENTANCE • The people gathered to return to the Lord. Hezekiah prayed for the people. "And the Lord heard Hezekiah and healed the people" (2 Chron. 30:20). When the people returned to the Lord and worshiped Him, the covenant relationship of love was reestablished. The people experienced great joy in their worship. In fact they decided to celebrate the feast seven more days because of their great joy. Their "practice" and "obedience" changed once the relationship with God was restored: "When all this had ended, the Israelites who were there went out to the towns of Judah, smashed the sacred stones and cut down the Asherah poles. They destroyed the high places and the altars throughout Judah and Benjamin and in Ephraim and Manasseh" (2 Chron. 31:1). During the next five months, the people "generously" brought tithes "of everything" to the Lord (see 2 Chron. 31:5). "When Hezekiah and his officials came and saw the heaps, they praised the Lord and blessed his people Israel" (2 Chron. 31:8).

Here is a summary of Hezekiah's work: "This is what Hezekiah did . . . what was good and right and faithful before the Lord his God. In everything that he undertook in the service of God's temple . . . he sought his God and worked wholeheartedly. And so he prospered" (2 Chron. 31:20-21).

ENCOUNTERING GOD IN PRAYER
Think about the joy in worship and the signs of revival that took place under Hezekiah's leadership. Does your church experience this kind of joy with the Lord in worship? If not, pray for your spiritual leaders as they guide your church to return to the Lord. Ask God to give your church a unity of mind to return to Him with all their hearts. Humble yourself before God in prayer. Ask God what you need to do to get ready for revival.

Day 3: Revival in the Church

When God comes in revival, He comes as a refiner's fire (see Mal. 3:2). A refiner's fire burns away all the impurities to leave pure metal. When God comes, He too burns away all the impurities and waste.

John the Baptist said Jesus baptized with the Holy Spirit and fire (Luke 3:16-17). People either came to Jesus or fought against Him. God exposes the attitude of the heart when He comes in revival. Because you were called to be "a people belonging to God" (1 Pet. 2:9), you cannot be neutral. Once you hear what God wants you to do, you must do it. You must either obey Him or suffer the consequences of rebellion. Individuals and churches cannot continue to do business as usual when God is calling them to revival and to be part of an awakening in the land.

◆ Read Jeremiah 8:5-7. Underline the things that were wrong with the response of God's people.

God came to His people (not the pagan nations of the world) and here is what He found.
His people:
- had turned away from Him
- clung to deceit
- refused to return
- did not say what is right
- did not repent of wickedness
- did whatever they wanted
- did not know God's requirements

Do any of these sound familiar to you? Even among God's people? The reason is found in Malachi 3:18. When God comes, He causes a division between those who will follow Him and those who will not. Do not be surprised if some people in your church oppose efforts supporting revival. According to Scripture, they do not like the light because it will expose their evil deeds (see John 3:19-21). Nevertheless, churches need revival.

MALACHI 3:1-2,5 • [1]"Suddenly the Lord you are seeking will come. . . . [2]But who can endure the day of his coming? Who can stand when he appears? For he will be like a refiner's fire or a launderer's soap."
[5]"So I will come near to you for judgment."

LUKE 3:16-17 • [6]One more powerful than I will come. . . . He will baptize you with the Holy Spirit and with fire. [17]His winnowing fork is in his hand to clear his threshing floor and to gather the wheat into his barn, but he will burn up the chaff with unquenchable fire.

JEREMIAH 8:5-7 • [5]"Why have these people turned away? . . . They cling to deceit; they refuse to return. [6]I have listened attentively, but they do not say what is right. No one repents of his wickedness saying, 'What have I done?' Each pursues his own course. . . . [7]But my people do not know the requirements of the Lord."

MALACHI 3:18 • You will again see the distinction between the righteous and the wicked, between those who serve God and those who do not.

JOHN 3:19-21 • [19]"This is the verdict: Light has come into the world, but men loved darkness instead of light because their deeds were evil. [20]Everyone who does evil hates the light, and will not come into the light for fear that his deeds will be exposed. [21]But whoever lives by the truth comes into the light, so that it may be seen plainly that what he has done has been done through God."

RESPONDING TO GOD AS A CHURCH • Because the church was still young when the New Testament was written, we do not have many details about corporate repentance. We mainly see the call for it in the New Testament. The Old Testament, however, is the foundation of our understanding about how God relates to His people. You have studied four examples of corporate revival. Let's review.

◆ Turn to each of the revivals listed below and briefly review the lessons. Place a check mark by each one after you have reviewed it.
❏ Ezra and Nehemiah (p. 24) ❏ Josiah and Hilkiah (p. 80)
❏ Asa and Azariah (p. 66) ❏ Hezekiah (p. 88)

We can see several factors that seem to be common to these corporate revival experiences.

CORPORATE REVIVAL EXPERIENCES
1. Led by one or more leaders, they began at the top with the leadership. Other leaders were drawn in as the revival spread.
2. In every case the people had experienced severe discipline and judgment from the Lord.
3. Most occurred on a scheduled time for "revival" or covenant renewal. These included the feasts of Trumpets, Tabernacles, and Passover.
4. All the people were expected to attend. This was serious business, no excuses were acceptable. The life of the nation depended on their response.
5. As part of these worship experiences, the leaders helped the people (1) remember what God had done for them in the past, (2) express worship and praise with rejoicing, and (3) offer offerings and sacrifices. They began with worship. After repentance, the joy of worship was great.
6. The Scriptures were a vital part of the experience. Through God's Word the people came to know God's requirements. They also understood the consequences if they did not return to the Lord.
7. The leaders and the people confessed and repented of their sins and the sins of their fathers before them.
8. The people demonstrated their repentance by removing idols, cleansing places of worship, and changing their ways.
9. The people did all these things wholeheartedly and with joy. They did not have to be forced into response.
10. God responded by cleansing, forgiving, restoring, and blessing His repentant people. God's presence returned to restore life to His people.

ENCOUNTERING GOD IN PRAYER
Ask God how He would like for you to pray for your church, for your pastor, and for other leaders in your church. Ask God what He wants you to do to prepare the way for corporate revival. Agree with God that you will do whatever He may ask of you and your church.

Day 4: Revival is God's Work

God is the One who revives His repentant people. Revival is an act of a sovereign God. We cannot cause a revival to take place. We cannot force God to act. We cannot "pray it down." God brings revival under His conditions and on His timetable. Yet, God wants us revived more than we do. In fact, God is the One who causes us to want to be revived. We come to God at His invitation.

◆ **Who takes the initiative to bring about revival? Check one.**

❏ I take the initiative.
❏ Our church body gets things started.
❏ God invites us to return to Him.
❏ My pastor is responsible.
❏ A prayer group prays revival down.
❏ Nobody; it is up to fate.

THE ROLE OF PRAYER • Do you remember God's four requirements for revival in 2 Chronicles 7:14? We humble ourselves, pray, turn from our wicked ways, and seek His face. Some people have noticed that united, visible, and extraordinary prayer has preceded every great revival in history. They have reached the conclusion that prayer is the secret to getting God to act. Many pray, however, and never experience revival.

Prayer is not just a religious activity. Prayer is a relationship between a person and God. But prayer alone does not cause revival to come. We pray because God has initiated a relationship with us. God invites us into His presence. When we pray, we enter into God's presence and come to know the heart and will of our Heavenly Father. In His presence in prayer, we become aware of our sinful condition. With a broken and contrite heart we cry out to God, and He calls us to repent of specific sins.

Prayer alone is *not* the key to revival. Humility is not enough. Seeking God's face is not enough either. All of these are important, and they lead to the ultimate requirement, repentance. Without repentance, revival will not take place. We must turn from our wicked ways, return to God, and live according to His ways. When we return to God, He has promised that He will return to us. He is a covenant keeping God—God keeps His promises.

◆ **Which of the following best describes the role of prayer in revival?**
❏ Prayer is a relationship with God through which we come to know what He wants from us. Then we respond to God in repentance.
❏ Prayer is a tool. When we get together and pray fervently claiming God's promises, we push Him into a corner. God has to send revival.
❏ Prayer is like magic words. If we come up with the right combination, "presto"—revival comes.
❏ Prayer is just one requirement on our checklist of things we have to do for revival. When we have prayed enough, we can check it off.

Prayer for revival is not a tool for manipulating God. It is not magic or just an activity to complete. Prayer is a relationship with God through which we respond to Him, come near to Him, and find Him. Prayer that results in genuine repentance is our part of the process. Then God keeps His promises!

How to Know When Revival Has Come • God said, "Return to me, and I will return to you" (Mal. 3:7). How can you know when revival has come? The way to know if you have returned is to see if God has returned to you. If you are still missing out on His presence and power, you have not yet met God's requirements. Your return (repentance) is not complete. When you experience God personally or corporately, you will never be the same. If you are still the same, whatever you have done, you have not encountered God. At a time like this, you need to go to God and ask Him what you still need to do in repentance.

◆ Which comes first?
❏ God returns to me.   ❏ I return to God.

God is waiting for you to draw near to Him. Repentance and revival, however, are not just a reform of behavior. Revival has not taken place unless a change of character has occurred, not unless a change of heart has taken place. When your love for the Lord compels you to obey Him and your heart's desire is to please Him, revival has occurred. The love relationship has been restored.

JEREMIAH 24:7 • "I will give them a heart to know me, that I am the Lord. They will be my people, and I will be their God, for they will return to me with all their heart."

EZEKIEL 36:22-30,36

²²"This is what the Sovereign Lord says: It is not for your sake, O house of Israel, that I am going to do these things, but for the sake of my holy name . . . ²³I will show the holiness of my great name . . . the name you have profaned among them. Then the nations will know that I am the Lord, declares the Sovereign Lord, when I show myself holy through you before their eyes.

²⁴"For I will take you out of the nations; I will gather you from all the countries and bring you back into your own land. ²⁵I will sprinkle clean water on you, and you will be clean; I will cleanse you from all your impurities and from all your idols. ²⁶I will give you a new heart and put a new spirit in you; I will remove from you your heart of stone and give you a heart of flesh. ²⁷And I will put my Spirit in you and move you to follow my decrees and be careful to keep my laws. ²⁸You will live in the land I gave your forefathers; you will be my people, and I will be your God. ²⁹I will save you from all your uncleanness. I will call for the grain and make it plentiful and will not bring famine upon you. ³⁰I will increase the fruit of the trees and the crops of the field, so that you will no longer suffer disgrace among the nations because of famine.

³⁶"Then the nations around you that remain will know that I the Lord have rebuilt what was destroyed and have replanted what was desolate. I the Lord have spoken, and I will do it."

ENCOUNTERING GOD IN PRAYER

Read Jeremiah 24:7. Ask God to give you a heart to know Him. Read the verses from Ezekiel 36. Listen to what God may want to say to you. Underline everything God says He will do in revival.

Day 5: Prepare the Way of the Lord

As you read through Ezekiel 36 yesterday, you found that these are some of the things God does when He brings revival:

☐ ☐ 1. He shows the holiness of His name
☐ ☐ 2. He sprinkles us with clean water and makes us clean.
☐ ☐ 3. He cleanses us from all impurities and all substitutes (idols).
☐ ☐ 4. He removes our stony hearts and gives tender hearts of flesh.
☐ ☐ 5. He puts a new spirit in us—His Spirit—and moves us to obey Him.
☐ ☐ 6. He saves us from all our uncleanness.
☐ ☐ 7. He restores what was taken away during His discipline and judgment.
☐ ☐ 8. He removes our disgrace among the nations.
☐ ☐ 9. He resettles our towns and rebuilds our ruined cities.

◆ Read back through the list. Place a check ✔ beside the ones you sense a need to experience. Draw an ✘ beside the ones you sense your church needs to experience. Circle the number of the ones you sense your town or city needs to experience.

Before God sent His Son Jesus to earth, God sent John the Baptist to prepare for Jesus. John prepared for the coming of the Messiah—the Anointed One. When Jesus comes again to take His bride (the church) to heaven for His wedding, the bride will have prepared herself (see Rev. 19:6-8). We need to prepare ourselves for the coming of the Lord—for His coming in revival and awakening and for His coming to take His bride away.

How do we prepare ourselves for the mighty movement of God through a people who have returned to Him?

◆ Read Luke 3:2-8 and circle things we can do to prepare.

◆ Read Malachi 4:1-2,5-6. What will the prophet do to prepare for the Lord's coming?

LUKE 3:2-8 • [2]The word of God came to John . . . [3]He went into all the country around the Jordan, preaching a baptism of repentance for the forgiveness of sins. [4]As is written in the book of the words of Isaiah the prophet: "A voice of one calling in the desert, 'Prepare the way for the Lord, make straight paths for him. [5]Every valley shall be filled in, every mountain and hill made low. The crooked roads shall become straight, the rough ways smooth. [6]And all mankind will see God's salvation.'"
[7]John said to the crowds coming out to be baptized by him, "You brood of vipers! Who warned you to flee from the coming wrath? [8]Produce fruit in keeping with repentance.

REVELATION 19:6-8 • [6]"Hallelujah! For our Lord God Almighty reigns. [7]Let us rejoice and be glad and give him glory! For the wedding of the Lamb has come and his bride has made herself ready. [8]Fine linen, bright and clean, was given her to wear." [Fine linen stands for the righteous acts of the saints.]

94

Spiritual awakening is the coming of God's life to people who were dead in sin. Spiritual awakening is the mighty sovereign work of God in saving masses of people. Spiritual awakening is a by-product of God's people getting their hearts and lives right with Him. It always has a powerful social impact resulting in serious reform. God wants to bring spiritual awakening to your community and nation. Is God waiting for you and your church?

MALACHI 4:1-2,5-6 • [1]"Surely the day is coming; it will burn like a furnace. All the arrogant and every evildoer will be stubble, and that day that is coming will set them on fire," says the Lord Almighty. "Not a root or a branch will be left to them. [2]But for you who revere my name, the sun of righteousness will rise with healing in its wings. And you will go out and leap like calves released from the stall."

[5]"See, I will send you the prophet Elijah before that great and dreadful day of the Lord comes. [6]He will turn the hearts of the fathers to their children, and the hearts of the children to their fathers; or else I will come and strike the land with a curse."

PSALM 139:1-4,23-24 • [1]O Lord, you have searched me and you know me. [2]You know when I sit and when I rise; you perceive my thoughts from afar. [3]You discern my going out and my lying down; you are familiar with all my ways. [4]Before a word is on my tongue you know it completely, O Lord.

[23]Search me, O God, and know my heart; test me and know my anxious thoughts. [24]See if there is any offensive way in me, and lead me in the way everlasting.

PSALM 86:11 • [11]Teach me your way, O Lord, and I will walk in your truth; give me an undivided heart, that I may fear your name.

ENCOUNTERING GOD IN PRAYER

Pray Psalm 139:1-4,23-24 and Psalm 86:11 to the Lord. Think seriously about your request. Meditate on the following questions. Ask the Lord to identify anything He wants you to do to prepare for His coming in revival or awakening.
- Are there things missing in your life (valleys) that need to be filled in?
- Are there spiritual strongholds, idols, or barriers (mountains) that need to be torn down?
- Are there any crooked ways that need to be straightened?
- Are there rough places (or relationships) that need to be made smooth?
- What must you do to demonstrate genuine repentance?
- Are there ways God wants you to turn your heart toward home (toward children or parents)?

Unit 6 Review: God Revives His Repentant People

◆ As a review of this unit, answer the following questions. If you need help, scan back through the unit for answers.

1. Fill in the blanks in Phases 6 and 7 below.
Phase 6: *God _____ His repentant people by restoring them to a _____ relationship with _____.*

Phase 7: *God exalts His Son _____ in His people and draws the lost to saving _____ in Him.*

2. Who takes the initiative in bringing revival?

_____

3. Which of the following is the primary role of prayer for revival? Check one.

❑ a. Prayer is a tool for us to claim God's promises and force Him to send revival in keeping with His promises.
❑ b. Prayer is a relationship through which God reveals what He wants us to do to return to Him.

4. Which of the following is the best way to tell when revival has come?

❑ a. Revival has come when God returns to us in power and we experience His presence, forgiveness, and healing.
❑ b. Revival has come when we complete all the things we think are required for God to send revival.

5. What statement, Scripture, or idea has been most meaningful to you in this unit? _____

_____

_____

6. Reword that statement, Scripture, or idea into a prayer response to God. _____

_____

_____

7. Write from memory Ephesians 3:20-21 describing God's glory in the church. _____

_____

_____

_____

_____

_____

8. Review all six memory verses and continue to keep God's Word in your heart.

9. Considering all that you have studied during the past six weeks, what is the most important thing you sense God has said to you? _____

_____

_____

_____

_____

Entering a Love Relationship with God

God created every person for a love relationship with Himself. Consider your relationship with God.

GOD'S INITIATIVE • God wants a love relationship with you. In fact He pursues that love relationship. Jesus said, "No one can come to me unless the Father who sent me draws him" (John 6:44). If you are feeling drawn to a love relationship with God, if you are feeling drawn to a relationship with Jesus, that is God working in you. God uses His love to draw you. "For God so loved the world that he gave his one and only Son, that whoever believes in him shall not perish but have eternal life. For God did not send his Son into the world to condemn the world, but to save the world through him" (John 3:16-17).

GOD'S INVITATION • God invites you to respond to Him: "The Spirit and the bride say, 'Come!' And let him who hears say, 'Come!' Whoever is thirsty, let him come; and whoever wishes, let him take the free gift of the water of life" (Rev. 22:17). Jesus is that "water of life." Jesus is your life. Jesus said, "I am the resurrection and the life. He who believes in me will live, even though he dies; and whoever lives and believes in me will never die" (John 11:25-26).

THE COST OF DISCIPLESHIP • For Jesus to be your life, you must die to self. Self must be spiritually put to death, so that Christ may take up residence in you and become your life. To be a disciple of Jesus is costly. It costs your self-life. Jesus said, "If anyone would come after me, he must deny himself and take up his cross and follow me. For whoever wants to save his life will lose it, but whoever loses his life for me will find it. What good will it be for a man if he gains the whole world, yet forfeits his soul?" (Matt. 16:24-26). Jesus wants to be absolute Lord of your life. He wants you to surrender everything to His rule (see Luke 14:33). Before you respond to God, count the cost. Keep in mind, though, Jesus said: "I have come that they

may have life, and have it to the full" (John 10:10). Having His life is worth any cost!

RESPONDING TO GOD'S INVITATION • Jesus' message from the beginning of His ministry was: "Repent and believe the good news!" (Mark 1:15). To repent, turn from your self-centered, sinful life and to Him. Then He becomes your life. You are born again. This response is not just a decision to make intellectually. The decision is not just some steps to follow or a prayer to pray. This is a spiritual death to self, allowing God to bring life by His presence.

If you are willing to die to self so that Christ may live in you:

• Agree with God that you are a sinner. Agree with Him that Jesus' death on the cross is your only hope of forgiveness.

• Ask God to forgive you of your sin and cleanse you by Jesus' blood.

• Thank God for loving you. Tell God about your love for Him.

• Surrender your will and your life to Christ's lordship —agree to obey Him in every area of your life.

• Accept God's free gift of salvation.

Experiencing God: Knowing and Doing the Will of God is another course coauthored by Henry Blackaby and Claude King. The individual and small-group studies help you and your church move into a deeper love relationship with God. It will help you learn to hear when God is speaking to you, to recognize where God is working and join Him, and to experience God doing through you what only God can do!

These course materials are being used by people around the world. There is a clear relationship between the seven realities of *Experiencing God* and the first phase of *God's Pattern for Revival and Spiritual Awakening* where God calls a people to be on mission with Him. The following statements from *Experiencing God* are some that have been helpful to people seeking to know and do God's will:

- Watch to see where God is at work and join Him.
- God reveals what He is about to do. The revelation is your invitation to join Him.
- You cannot stay where you are and go with God.
- Understanding what God is about to do where you are is more important than telling God what you want to do for Him.
- If you have trouble hearing God speak, you are in trouble at the very heart of your Christian experience.
- Knowing God's voice comes from an intimate love relationship with God.
- God develops character to match the assignment.
- Any assignment from God is an important assignment.
- You never find God asking persons to dream up what they want to do for Him.
- God takes the initiative to involve people in His work.
- The moment God speaks is God's timing.
- God reveals Himself to increase my faith.
- God reveals His ways so you can accomplish His purposes.
- God is love. His will is always best.

- God is all-knowing. His directions are always right.
- God is all-powerful. He can enable you to do His will.
- You never discover truth. Truth is revealed.
- Understanding spiritual truth does not lead you to an encounter with God; it *is* the encounter with God.
- Prayer is a relationship, not just a religious activity.
- Truth is a Person.
- You cannot know the truth of your circumstance until you have heard from God.
- Apart from the body of Christ, you cannot fully know God's will for your relationship to the body.
- What you do reveals what you believe about God, regardless of what you say.
- God is interested in absolute surrender.
- Obedience is costly to you and to those around you.
- "It" never works. He works!
- The God who initiates His work in a relationship with you is the One Himself who guarantees to complete it.
- A church comes to know the will of God when the whole body understands what Christ—the Head—is telling them.
- The Head does the convincing on His timetable.
- When a church allows God's presence and activity to be expressed, a watching world will be drawn to Him.
- Every congregation is a world missions strategy center.

For further details about any of the following resources from LifeWay Press, call 1-800-458-2772 or check with your local bookstore.
- *Experiencing God: Knowing and Doing the Will of God*
- *Experiencing God Leader's Guide*
- *The 7 Realities of Experiencing God* (video series)
- *Experiencing God Audiotapes*—twelve 45-minute messages
Order these materials using the tear-off order card on this book.